PRIMAL BLUEPRINT

Healthy Sauces, Dressings & Toppings

MARK SISSON
WITH JENNIFER MEIER

Primal Blueprint Healthy Sauces, Dressings & Toppings

Library of Congress Control Number: 2012918932

Library of Congress Cataloging-in-Publication Data
Sisson, Mark, 1953–

Primal Blueprint Healthy Sauces, Dressings & Toppings / Mark Sisson with Jennifer Meier

ISBN 978-0984755158
1. Cooking 2. Health 3. Diet 4. Low Carb

Editor/Project Manager: Aaron Fox
Assistant Editors: Jessica Tudzin, Brad Kearns
Editorial Assistant: Gail Kearns
Design/Layout: Kristin Roybal
Cover Design: Caroline De Vita

For more information about the Primal Blueprint, please visit www.primalblueprint.com
For information on quantity discounts, please call 888-774-6259

Publisher: Primal Nutrition, Inc.
23805 Stuart Ranch Rd. Suite 145
Malibu, CA 90265

acknowledgments

Mark Sisson: This book was only made possible by the vibrant community found at my blog, MarksDailyApple.com. The daily feedback I get each week from tens of thousands of readers trying to live healthy, Primal lifestyles in the modern world is what inspired this cookbook. Many thanks to each and every one of you.

My co-author Jennifer Meier deserves enormous credit for bringing our vision for this cookbook to life with delicious original recipes (many of which have become staples in my own kitchen), and with all the incredible photographs she took. With the hundreds of sauces and dressings she tested in preparation for this cookbook it was quite a sticky undertaking, but she handled it like a pro.

Aaron Fox, my general manager and MarksDailyApple.com webmaster was instrumental in coordinating the efforts of everyone in the project, and was the main copy editor of the cookbook. Jessica Tudzin, Primal Blueprint Publishing's new editor, also provided valuable editing support. My ace designer Kristin Roybal came through yet again with a fabulous interior design and layout. Caroline De Vita did a tremendous job with the book cover design. Finally, much gratitude to Brad Kearns for his excellent insights, and to Gail Kearns who assumed the task of divining all the macronutrient breakdowns and metric unit measurements.

Special thanks to my wife Carrie and children Devyn and Kyle for their love and support.

Jennifer Meier: It has again been a huge pleasure to work with Mark Sisson and the entire Primal team to develop this cookbook. Their inexhaustible quest to find real solutions to the health issues of today has forever changed the way I cook. I also want to thank the readers at MarksDailyApple.com. Your enthusiasm for truly delicious food inspires me as a chef. Every recipe in this book was created with you in mind.

contents

🥛 Indicates recipe contains dairy

Salad Dressing 113

Dips, Condiments and Garnishes 165

introduction

If you know how to grill steak, sauté vegetables, and toss raw greens, then you know how to cook a basic meal. The problem is *basic* can get boring really fast. Luckily, there are dozens of easy ways to add excitement and variety to your daily dishes.

Here's how it works: buy your favorite protein and a selection of brightly colored vegetables. Then turn to any page in this cookbook. Guaranteed, you'll find a yummy sauce, dressing, condiment, or seasoning that will take the meal you're planning from simple to sensational, whether it's with a bowl of spicy salsa, a smear of tangy barbecue sauce, or a delicate drizzle of white wine and butter.

Many of the recipes in this book are inspired by the classics— Béarnaise sauce, Thousand Island dressing, Dijon mustard—but with a lighter, fresher twist. And others, such as the Coconut-Almond Marinade (page 241) and the Lemon-Ginger Dressing (page 150), are creative and bold. But they all add nutrients to your meal, using only Primal-approved ingredients and nothing objectionable. That means no flour, grains, legumes, added sugar, or trans or partially hydrogenated fats. It also means little or no dairy. For those who do not consume dairy, we have indicated those few recipes that contain it with a symbol of a milk carton.

My book, *The Primal Blueprint*, has empowered thousands of people to make necessary lifestyle changes with minimal sacrifice and little chance of failure. *Primal Blueprint Healthy Sauces, Dressings & Toppings* is an extension of that empowerment. Even if you don't already follow a Primal/paleo lifestyle, and you're simply searching for ways to eat better by going on a gluten-free, dairy-free, or low-carb diet, this cookbook is for you. You'll find easy cooking techniques to help you reach your nutritional goals with more than 120 no-fail ways to boost the flavor of anything and everything you eat.

Although they are based on an eating strategy that emulates the hunter-gatherer diet of our ancestors, these recipes are for the modern palate, with innovative and lively flavors. This is the primary focus of Primal eating: foods that are both delicious and nutritious, made from quality sources of protein, fresh vegetables and fruit, and satisfying essential fats. Our hunter-gatherer genes are programmed to crave these life-sustaining foods. Stray too far into low-fat/high-carb territory and you'll find that weight loss, high energy, and a strong immune system will always be elusive.

A diet heavy in grains (wheat, barley, corn, etc.), legumes (peanut, soy, and other beans), simple sugars, and trans and hydrogenated fats and oils makes most people sick and sluggish over time. These aren't the foods our genes are historically programmed to eat. Neither are processed convenience foods. Lucky were our hunter-gatherer ancestors who did not have them as an option.

If you've been turning to commercial sauces, dressings, condiments, and seasonings to enhance your meals, it's likely you've been disappointed. The flavor is usually nothing to rave about. Even worse, their ingredients put your long-term health at risk. When you open a bottle of store-bought salad dressing, you are more than likely pouring preservatives, sweeteners, and industrial oils onto your otherwise healthful salad. Indeed, there are few things you can do in the kitchen as dangerous as pouring these poisons masquerading as dressings and sauces onto your food.

This cookbook is a better solution, especially if convenience is important to you. Making homemade sauce from scratch can be intimidating, but the recipes in this cookbook prove that making a great one is possible, even if you're short on time, cooking experience, or both. While all the recipes are infinitely versatile, they are also simple to prepare, and many can be made rather quickly. You'll learn tricks for thickening sauces, discover a variety of healthful oils for salad dressings, and see how easy it is to stock your spice drawer with fresh, homemade rubs.

Every recipe also comes with a macronutrient profile (courtesy of Paleotrack.com) so you can get an idea of the nutritional breakdown at a glance. Keep in mind that all calculations are approximations, with all figures rounded to the nearest whole number. With these macronutrient profiles you'll be able to select recipes that are appropriate for your and your family's health goals.

With this cookbook, and *The Primal Blueprint* as your guide, you're well on your way to reaching all your health and fitness goals, one delicious meal at a time.

HOP ONLINE AND VISIT MARKSDAILYAPPLE.COM FOR HUNDREDS OF RECIPES AND LIFESTYLE TIPS, AND TO JOIN THE CONVERSATION ABOUT HOW TO LIVE PRIMALLY IN THE MODERN WORLD.

the good, the bad, and the not so horrible

In an ideal world, every meal would be made from local, seasonal, organic, pastured, grass-fed, or wild ingredients with a perfect ratio of essential fatty acids.

If you can get pretty close to this most or some of the time, keep it up. Great chefs insist on fresh, high-quality ingredients. As a home cook, you should insist on this, too. Shop at farmers markets, try growing your own fruits and vegetables, or buy what's ripe and in season at the grocery store. Refresh your spice drawer every few months, and always keep fresh herbs on hand. Buy the highest quality meat you can, choose butter from grass-fed cows if possible, and make your own stock instead of buying it. Being choosy about what you buy makes everything taste better.

If sourcing such ingredients is not realistic for you on a regular or even semi-regular basis, don't despair. With this cookbook, even less-than-ideal Primal foods—such as grain-fed beef, farm-raised fish, non-organic produce, and starchy tubers—can be transformed into more acceptable choices.

By pairing a Primal sauce, dressing, or other flavor enhancer with whatever you happen to be eating, you'll automatically add more vitamins, minerals, antioxidants, fiber, and omega-3 fatty acids. First, determine what on your plate is less than ideal. Then, look for a recipe that will balance out the bad with a whole lot of good.

Less than ideal	Primal solution
Less-expensive, tough cuts of meat	Pick any marinade to flavor and tenderize the meat
Grain-fed beef	Trim off the fat then add back healthier fat by topping the cooked meat with flavored butter like Bacon Chive Butter (page 200)
Farm-raised salmon	Balance out the overload of omega-6 by using a dressing with an extremely low omega-6 profile like Macadamia Oil Dressing (page 156)
Conventional chicken	Reduce omega-6 fatty acids that are concentrated in the fat by pulling off the skin. Combat lack of flavor and tough texture with a yogurt-based Indian Marinade (page 243). Or, top the chicken with Coconut-Shallot Sauce (page 84) made from butter, coconut milk, and olive oil
Iceberg lettuce	Add healthful fat and vitamins to this low-nutrient green with a powerhouse like Creamy Avocado Dressing (page 146)
Lack of dark, leafy greens	Top meat, chicken, or fish with Creamy Arugula Sauce or Arugula-Watercress Pesto (pages 76 and 74)
Lack of brightly colored vegetables	Top meat or seafood with a tasty and visually appealing Roasted Red Pepper Pesto (page 70), Bell Pepper Sauce (page 68) or Carrot Salsa (page 96)
Mealy, bland out-of-season tomatoes	Turn them into a fiery Tomato Salsa (page 94)
Mashed potatoes	Instead of adding to the starch-fest with flour-thickened gravy, serve Almost Traditional Turkey Gravy (page 40) or Onion Gravy (page 46)
Milk Chocolate	Wean yourself off this sugary treat by combining it with antioxidant-rich Dark Chocolate Pudding Sauce (page 104) or Dark Chocolate Coconut Sauce (page 102)

know your ingredients

If you've read *The Primal Blueprint* or have visited my website, MarksDaily-Apple.com, you know all about stocking a Primal kitchen. If you're new to Primal eating or need a refresher, the list of common Primal ingredients provided here is an indispensable guide.

For the best possible cooking results, read through this list before you try any of the recipes in this book.

Butter   All butter used for these recipes should be unsalted so you can control the seasoning. Ideally, cook with grass-fed butter, although grain-fed butter is still a better option than conventional cooking fats like vegetable oil or margarine. Ghee, a clarified butter that has no lactose or dairy proteins, is another excellent choice. It's great for cooking and can be used in place of regular butter.

Coconut Milk   The recipes in this book call for full-fat (not low-fat), unsweetened, canned coconut milk. Canned coconut milk is richer and thicker and better for cooking than the refrigerated coconut milk sold in cartons for drinking. Once opened and transferred to an airtight container, canned coconut milk will stay fresh about a week in the refrigerator. If you don't use the full can for a recipe, pour the remainder into a smoothie or your morning cup of coffee.

Flour Alternatives   While nut and coconut flours have their place in the Primal kitchen (primarily for baking) they aren't the best for thickening sauces. If you're trying to thicken a sauce or gravy, there are many other Primal-approved options to try, each with pros and cons.

Reducing   An ideal thickening option because you don't have to add any additional ingredients. As sauce simmers without a lid it will naturally reduce, gradually thickening the sauce somewhat. Reducing also intensifies the flavor. This is usually a good thing, but can make some sauces turn out too salty.

Fats Adding butter, coconut milk, or whole cream can help thicken sauces, especially if you reduce the sauce after adding them.

Puréed Vegetables Steamed or sautéed, puréed vegetables (such as parsnips, onion, mushrooms, and squash) can add texture to a thin sauce. They will, however, impart their flavor to whatever you're cooking.

Arrowroot Mix 2 teaspoons (10 ml) of arrowroot with 2 teaspoons (10 ml) cold water per 1 cup (250 ml) of hot sauce, gravy, or stock. It will thicken the liquid without affecting the flavor. Make sure to add the arrowroot at the very end of the cooking process; if boiled too long, the sauce will thin out again.

Tapioca Starch/Flour Mix 1 tablespoon (15 ml) of tapioca starch with 1 tablespoon (15 ml) of cold water per 1 cup (250 ml) of hot sauce or gravy or stock. If this doesn't make the sauce thick enough, add more, up to double the amount. Tapioca is a fantastic thickener, but with a somewhat gummy texture. Make sure to add it at the very end of the cooking process; if boiled too long, the sauce will thin out again.

Almond Butter Smooth, unsalted, raw almond butter does a decent job of thickening cream-based sauces. It gives the sauce a slightly nutty flavor. To use, whisk 2 tablespoons (30 ml) of almond butter with 1 tablespoon (15 ml) of melted butter over medium heat. Slowly pour the gravy or sauce or cream into the almond butter while whisking.

Egg Yolk A nutritious but tricky thickener. If whisked egg yolks are added directly to a hot sauce, you'll end up with scrambled eggs. Instead, slowly whisk a few tablespoons (45 ml) of hot sauce, gravy, or stock into the bowl of egg yolks. Then, slowly add this mixture back into the sauce. Heat over low, stirring as the sauce thickens. Try using three whisked egg yolks per 1 cup (250 ml) of sauce, gravy, or stock.

Herbs Herbs are one of the easiest ways to add flavor to a meal, but in their dried form they rarely have enough flavor to be worthwhile. Most fresh herbs will keep longer if you gently wrap them in a thin cloth or paper towel, enclose them in a plastic bag, and refrigerate. The exception is basil, which keeps best in a jar of water at room temperature.

Nuts Overindulging in nuts heavy in omega-6 can spiral you towards pro-inflammatory processes—not good. But in moderation nuts can add flavor and texture to sauces like pesto.

Oils More and more oil options are springing up in the grocery aisle. At first glance, many of these new oils seem like they'd be good for you. But how do you know? We've done the hard work for you, analyzing and cooking with them all. Keep these oils in your kitchen, and get rid of the rest:

Avocado Oil With a fatty acid profile similar to that of olive oil and a light avocado flavor, this oil can be an occasional change of pace for salad dressing and low-heat cooking.

Coconut Oil This shelf-stable oil heats up well and is a near-perfect source of healthful saturated fat. Look for unrefined, organic virgin oil. Note that it will add a light coconut flavor to whatever you're cooking.

Nut Oils Used in moderation (a splash in a salad dressing or marinade), nut oils can add interesting flavor. Macadamia is one of our favorites, for its sweet nutty flavor. Also, unlike most nut oils, it's highly shelf-stable and resistant to heat-induced oxidation.

Olive Oil A great addition to your diet and not just for salad dressing. Good extra virgin olive oil that's stored away from heat and light is decently resistant to heat-incurred oxidative damage. So don't worry too much about cooking with olive oil, as long as you're buying olive oil of a decent quality. Good olive oil is often bitter, pungent, and spicy. It has character. If your bottle of olive oil is smooth and flavorless, it might not have as many polyphenols, the antioxidant compounds that make the oil so good for you.

Red Palm Oil and Palm Oil Palm oil is an acquired taste, but it's brimming with antioxidants and can reduce oxidized LDL in humans. A great choice as a primary cooking oil.

Sesame Oil   Adds unique, irreplaceable flavor. Not for everyday use, but a little here and there is fine.

Sunflower Oil   A good choice if you need flavorless oil for recipes like making mayonnaise. Just be sure to read the label carefully and buy only cold-pressed (which preserves vitamin E and reduces oxidation), high-oleic/high-stearic sunflower oil.

Salt   Unless otherwise noted, all salt used in these recipes is kosher salt. The coarse texture clings to food well and it's easier to handle if you're adding a pinch here and there. Also, most kosher salt is free of additives. Sea salt is a perfect salt to sprinkle on a dish after it's cooked, especially meat. The recipes in this cookbook don't go overboard with salt and call for just enough to punch up the flavor.

Spices   You've probably heard it before, and it's true: old spices don't have much more flavor than sawdust. What's old? Sniff the jar; if there's no aroma coming from the spice, there probably won't be any flavor either. Make an effort to buy whole spices from a trusted source, and grind them yourself; you'll be shocked by how much more flavor and aroma they have. Many spices have extremely high ORAC (Oxygen Radical Absorbance Capacity) scores, making them among the most potent antioxidants in nature.

Stock   There is simply no replacement for homemade stock. Not in terms of flavor and definitely not in terms of the health benefits. Animal bones are loaded with good things (marrow, collagen, magnesium, and calcium, to name a few), and if you make your own stock using bones, those nutrients will be in every sip of stock. Homemade stock also has a rich, meaty flavor and isn't overly salty.

If you haven't yet stocked your freezer with homemade stock (chicken and beef), get busy! This easy recipe for chicken stock will get you started. It's deeply flavorful and tastes a whole lot better than any canned stock. »

Homemade Chicken Stock

While you can make stock from just bones, using a whole chicken adds more flavor. Plus, you get to eat the chicken afterwards.

4 to 5 pound (2 kg) chicken, cut into 8 pieces (giblets removed). If you can find some chicken feet, throw those in too.

1 gallon (4 L) cold water

1 large onion, peeled and quartered

4 celery ribs, cut into chunks

2 carrots, peeled and cut into chunks

2 bay leaves

3 to 4 whole black peppercorns

1 teaspoon (5 ml) salt

Place the chicken in a deep, narrow stockpot that holds the chicken snugly and doesn't require much more than 1 gallon (4 L) of water to cover the chicken.

Add the rest of the ingredients. Bring the uncovered pot to a boil then reduce the heat so the water is only simmering. Skim the foam off the top.

Keep the water at a simmer for about four hours.

Strain all the solids out of the stock. Cool the stock to room temperature. Refrigerate until the fat becomes solid on the surface. Spoon off the solidified fat then freeze the stock in 1 cup (250 ml) quantities for future use. For the best flavor, use frozen stock within one to two months.

Sweeteners In moderation, raw honey is a decent choice when a recipe needs a little sweetening. Fresh, ripe berries and other fruits can also be used to add sweetness.

Vinegar Another grocery aisle overflowing with choices is the one that contains vinegar. For the most part, you're safe to experiment freely to find your favorite. Higher-priced vinegars often do have more complex flavors and less of an acidic bite. Sherry, red wine, balsamic, unseasoned rice, and apple cider vinegar are a few favorites.

helpful kitchen tools

A cutting board, a few sharp knives, and a small set of quality pots and pans are a necessity in the kitchen. Beyond that, there's not a whole lot more that you absolutely must have. However, investing in a few gadgets and tools will make cooking a whole lot easier, and definitely more fun.

Mesh strainer   The easiest way to separate liquids from solids.

Whisk   Works better than a fork every time.

Small jars with lids   Instead of whisking your salad dressing ingredients, try shaking them. Glass jars are handy for storing dressings and condiments, too.

Blender   Great for mixing small amounts of ingredients and for giving sauces, dressings, and marinades a smoother texture than you typically can get from a food processor.

Food processor   Will save you tons of chopping time and mixes ingredients together with ease.

Kitchen shears   Instead of using a knife to chop fresh herbs, just cut them with shears. Also handy for trimming and cutting meat.

helpful cooking tips

Fat drippings and crispy bits, typically left behind in the pan after cooking meat, are loaded with flavor that can easily be captured in your homemade sauces. We recommend that you avoid non-stick pans, however, as they drastically reduce the yield that copper, cast iron, or stainless steel pans provide.

No matter what type of meat (or fish) you're cooking, the following method will make for a richly flavored sauce:

- After searing or pan-frying the meat, remove it from the pan.
- Pour off all but a few teaspoons of fat in the pan.
- *Optional:* Sauté shallot or mushrooms in the remaining fat.

- Add enough liquid (stock, wine, or coconut milk all work well) to just cover the bottom of the pan.
- Boil the liquid until it reduces by half. While it boils, use a spoon or spatula to loosen the bits of meat stuck to the pan.
- Turn off the heat, and stir in a tablespoon or two of butter, whole cream, or coconut milk to give the sauce more texture.
- *Optional:* Add a flavoring such as fresh herbs, salt, black pepper, capers, a squeeze of lemon, or mustard.

Salad, of course, is one of the easiest and healthiest meals on the planet. Grab a big bowl, throw in handfuls of greens, vegetables, and protein, pour dressing on top, and have at it. My all-time favorite lunch, one that I eat most days of the week, is salad. With so many different combinations of greens, veggies, and proteins to choose from, it's impossible to get tired of it.

One thing I do get tired of, though, is the same dressing day after day. Olive oil whisked with fresh lemon juice and a pinch of sea salt is a favorite standby, but we all need variety. In the chapter on dressings, you'll find a wide array of oils, vinegars, and seasonings with which to experiment. From rich and creamy to bold and tangy, every type of flavor is covered. It's likely that the recipes will inspire you to start concocting even more creative dressings. When they do, keep these tips in mind:

- To taste test salad dressing, dip a lettuce leaf into it instead of a spoon. Sipping salad dressing straight doesn't always indicate how good it will taste over greens.
- To revive wilted greens, soak in ice water for fifteen minutes.
- Make sure your greens are totally dry. Excess water diminishes the flavor of dressing. Invest in a salad spinner or give greens time to air dry by spreading them out on a towel. Experiment with all sorts of greens. Not only will this add more nutrients to your diet, you'll also discover that certain greens taste best with certain dressings. Heavy greens can handle thick, creamy dressings; lighter greens like arugula do better with a simple vinaigrette.

- When tossing a salad, start by adding just a little bit of dressing. You can always add more dressing, but adding too much will make the greens limp and soggy. Consider using your hands to toss a salad instead of tongs, and gently massage the dressing into the leaves.
- As a first step, combine any salt and garlic, shallot, or onion in the recipe with any vinegar or lemon juice, and then let them sit for ten to thirty minutes before whisking together. The salt will dissolve, and the garlic and shallot will become softer with a mellower bite.

If you're going to take the time to make your own spice blends, then do it right. Use whole seeds and grind them yourself. As you grind spices, the aroma will take over your kitchen. When was the last time that happened when you opened a bottled of store-bought, pre-ground spice?

As for grinding, coffee grinders work great on spice. Just don't use the same grinder to make coffee the next morning, or your morning brew will taste strangely like cumin and pepper. Or go the traditional route, and use a mortar and pestle to grind spices slowly by hand.

Toasting whole spices in a dry pan releases their essential oils and adds more fragrance to the finished dish. Before grinding, place whole spices in a sauté pan over medium heat, and toast until fragrant and very lightly browned, about three to five minutes.

Because it's hard to go wrong, marinades are another great way to experiment with flavor. Rarely does a marinade completely overpower and ruin a meal. Usually the worst that happens is the meat ends up with less flavor than you'd like. Combine a fat (usually oil), an acidic element (vinegar, citrus or wine), and a flavoring (garlic or any other fresh or dried herb or spice), and you've got a marinade.

You can marinate for hours, but often this isn't necessary. Instead, just marinate for thirty minutes at room temperature, not in the refrigerator. This gives the meat plenty of flavor and also helps meat cook evenly since the center isn't cold from refrigeration. Another myth is that meat has to be swimming in a large quantity of liquid marinade. A marinade that is more like a paste that can be brushed over meat works just as well, if not better, at flavoring proteins.

Olive oil is often the oil of choice in marinades, but it's worth considering others that stand up well to heat. I like grilling with coconut oil, and though you might imagine otherwise, it doesn't impart a strong coconut flavor.

An acidic element like vinegar, wine, or citrus is also found in most marinades. Acids heighten flavor and can help to break down the tough bonds holding proteins together, tenderizing the meat in the process. Some dairy products, such as plain yogurt or buttermilk, are also acidic enough to tenderize meat. This method works especially well with chicken or lamb. However, do be aware that too much time in any type of acidic marinade can have an opposite affect on meat, making it tougher, or giving it an unappetizing mushy texture.

When flavoring a marinade, go bold. Don't be shy about throwing in loads of garlic, ginger, onions, hot peppers, fresh herbs, or aromatic spices. Marinades with herbs such as rosemary, thyme, oregano, basil, or parsley and garlic are also thought to help reduce the carcinogenic compounds produced by grilling.

storing what you cook

To make meals a whole lot easier to get on the table, consider carving out some time on a weekend to stock up. Make a few double batches of sauce for the freezer, stock your fridge with condiments like homemade ketchup, mustard, and relish and add some new spice blends to your spice drawer. Share your bounty with others—homemade sauces, condiments, and spice blends make great gifts when stored in decorative glass jars.

Many of the sauces in this cookbook (with the exceptions of things like salsa and raw-egg emulsions like béarnaise and hollandaise) will freeze well.

- Food must be completely cooled before freezing.
- Smaller portions freeze more quickly and help maintain good flavor and texture.
- Plastic freezer bags are great for storing sauces. They take up less room in the freezer than containers and are easy to label.
- If using freezer bags, remove all the air from the bag before sealing.
- Always label the container or freezer bag with the name of the contents and the date it was made.
- Most cooked food tastes best if eaten within three months of being frozen.
- To reheat, place in the refrigerator to defrost first. Or speed things up by placing a plastic freezer bag filled with sauce directly into a pot of hot water. Once the contents soften and break into pieces, pour out into a saucepan for stovetop heating.

Salad dressing can also be made ahead of time, so you have several instant options whenever you toss a salad. Kept in the refrigerator, most homemade dressings taste best if eaten within a week, or sooner if they contain perishable ingredients like mayonnaise, sour cream, or eggs. Many oils, especially coconut oil, will congeal in the fridge and separate from the other dressing ingredients. To bring the dressing back to an emulsified state, just whisk or shake briskly. Or heat in a microwave for ten seconds to liquefy.

Whole spices can be kept for up to a year, occasionally longer. They don't necessarily go bad, they just won't add any flavor to your food. Ground spices usually lose their potency within six months. The best way to know if spices are still fresh is to stick your nose in the bottle. If you don't detect a scent, it's time to toss them. To keep spices fresh as long as possible, don't store them directly next to the stove or oven. Heat destroys their essential oils.

With these useful tips and tricks you are prepared to begin making your own healthy sauces, dressings and toppings today!

QUICK AND EASY COMBINATIONS

Grilled pork chop over greens with Basil-Lime Dressing (page 134)

Mixed greens with chicken and Blue Cheese Vinaigrette (page 122)

Steamed or grilled salmon with a side of Carrot Salsa (page 96)

*Grilled or pan-seared flank steak with sautéed bell peppers and
Coconut-Cilantro Pesto (page 72)*

Pan-seared fish with sautéed Swiss chard smothered in Coconut-Shallot Sauce (page 84)

Grated and steamed cauliflower topped with sautéed shrimp and Tomato-Coconut Curry Sauce (page 90)

*Pan-roasted pork chop with sautéed spinach and a spoonful of
Fennel-Olive Tapenade (page 80)*

*Grilled steak and thinly sliced, sautéed zucchini topped with
Marinara Sauce (page 58)*

Roasted vegetables dressed with Minty Caper Sauce (page 78)

*Grilled chicken and steamed broccoli drizzled with
Mornay Sauce (page 36)*

Pot roast with sweet potatoes and Olive Gremolata (page 198)

*Sautéed chicken breast and steamed cauliflower topped with
Quick Mushroom Sauce (page 50)*

Grilled steak with sautéed mushrooms and
Roasted Red Pepper Pesto (page 70)

Fish with wakame seaweed, sliced red pepper, and grated carrot salad
tossed with Sesame-Coconut Dressing (page 148)

Grilled or steamed salmon and roasted carrots topped with
Spicy Poblano Sauce (page 66)

Chicken and broccoli sautéed in Stir-Fry Sauce (page 92)

Roast turkey or chicken with steamed, puréed root vegetable and
Almost Traditional Turkey Gravy (page 40)

Pan-fried or broiled white fish with roasted cauliflower and a spoonful
of Veracruz Sauce (page 64)

Thinly sliced, sautéed zucchini with Bolognese Sauce (page 55)

Beef sautéed with Green Curry Paste (page 223) and simmered with vegetables in coconut milk

*Pan-seared fish with sautéed mushrooms and red peppers, topped with
Creamy Arugula Sauce (page 76)*

*Scrambled eggs garnished with sliced tomatoes and
Arugula-Watercress Pesto (page 74)*

SAUCES

hollandaise sauce

You could stand over a stove whisking this sauce and praying that the egg yolks don't scramble, but why, when you can make this foolproof version in a blender? Make this classic sauce right before serving and pour over eggs, salmon, steak, and vegetables.

Makes 1 cup (250 ml), serves 8
Time in the kitchen: 10 minutes

3 egg yolks

2 tablespoons (30 ml) lemon juice

¼ teaspoon (1 ml) salt

12 tablespoons (175 ml) unsalted butter, cut into small chunks

Place egg yolks, lemon juice, and salt in blender. Let sit.

Heat the butter until it's completely melted and foamy. Use a spoon to skim as much of the white foam off the top as possible.

Blend the egg yolks and lemon juice on medium-high for twenty seconds. Remove the insert in the middle of the blender lid and with the blade running slowly pour in the warm melted butter.

Blend on high until a thick, creamy sauce forms, about forty seconds.

Suggested uses

Pour over lox, asparagus, or poached eggs.

macronutrient profile (per serving)
2 tbsp (30 ml) per serving

	Grams	Calories	%-Cals
Calories		177	
Fat	19	170	96%
Saturated	12	104	59%
Polyunsaturated	1	8	4%
Monounsaturated	5	47	27%
Carbohydrate	1	2	1%
Dietary Fiber	0		
Protein	1	5	3%

béarnaise sauce

Béarnaise is just like Hollandaise (page 30) except the preparation is a little fussier, and it has the anise-like flavor of tarragon. White wine intensifies the flavor of the sauce, but is entirely optional in this version.

Makes 1 cup (250 ml), serves 8
Time in the kitchen: 15 minutes

3 egg yolks

¼ cup (60 ml) dry white wine (optional)

¼ cup (60 ml) white wine vinegar

1 small shallot, finely chopped

2 tablespoons (30 ml) finely chopped fresh tarragon

8 tablespoons (125 ml) unsalted butter, cut into small chunks

1 teaspoon (5 ml) lemon juice

Season to taste with salt

Place the egg yolks in a blender. Let sit.

Bring wine, vinegar, shallot, and 1 tablespoon (15 ml) of the tarragon to a gentle simmer in a saucepan until the liquid is almost entirely reduced and only about 1 tablespoon (15 ml) of liquid remains.

Strain the liquid through a fine mesh sieve, pressing on the solids to release all the liquid.

Heat the butter until it's completely melted and foamy. Use a spoon to skim as much of the white foam off the top as possible.

Pour the vinegar liquid into the blender with the egg yolks. Blend on high for twenty seconds.

Remove the insert in the middle of the lid, and with the blade running slowly pour in the warm butter. Blend until a creamy sauce forms, about forty seconds.

Pour sauce into a bowl and stir in lemon juice, remaining tarragon, and salt to taste.

macronutrient profile (per serving)
2 tbsp (30 ml) per serving

	Grams	Calories	%-Cals
Calories		127	
Fat	13	119	94%
Saturated	8	71	56%
Polyunsaturated	1	7	5%
Monounsaturated	4	34	27%
Carbohydrate	1	3	2%
Dietary Fiber	0		
Protein	1	5	4%

Suggested uses

Drizzle over steak and lamb chops, or serve as a dip for shrimp.

horseradish sauce

Creamy, spicy, and the perfect topping for prime rib, pot roast, and steak. If you can find fresh horseradish root, use it instead of a jar of prepared horseradish for a spicier, cleaner flavor. If you don't eat dairy, blend chunks of peeled horseradish root in a food processor with vinegar and a little bit of water for a pungent garnish.

Makes 1 cup (250 ml), serves 8
Time in the kitchen: 5 minutes, plus 3 hours to chill

1 cup (250 ml) sour cream

4 tablespoons (60 ml) peeled, finely grated horseradish root

2 teaspoons (10 ml) white wine vinegar

Season to taste with salt

To grate the horseradish, use a microplane grater or the small holes on a box grater.

Combine all ingredients for the horseradish sauce in a small bowl.

Refrigerate several hours for the flavors to meld.

Suggested uses

Serve with beef roasts, use as a dip for raw veggies, or stir into puréed cauliflower.

macronutrient profile (per serving)
2 tbsp (30 ml) per serving

	Grams	Calories	%-Cals
Calories		58	
Fat	6	51	88%
Saturated	3	29	51%
Polyunsaturated	0	2	4%
Monounsaturated	2	14	23%
Carbohydrate	1	5	8%
Dietary Fiber	0		
Protein	1	3	4%

mornay sauce

Mornay is a cheese sauce that is typically thickened with flour. As it turns out, almond butter thickens this sauce beautifully and adds a subtle nutty flavor. Kids will love this sauce poured over veggies.

Makes 1 cup (250 ml), serves 8
Time in the kitchen: 20 minutes

¾ cup (175 ml) whipping cream

2 tablespoons (30 ml) butter

1 tablespoon (15 ml) smooth, unsalted, raw almond butter

1 cup (250 ml) grated cheese (such as cheddar)

Pinch of grated nutmeg

Gently warm the cream over medium-low heat.

In a separate saucepan, melt the butter over medium heat. Whisk in the almond butter.

Slowly pour the heated cream into the almond butter and bring to a gentle boil. Stir continuously with a spatula, scraping the bottom so the sauce doesn't stick to the pan.

Simmer three minutes then slowly stir in the cheese. Add the nutmeg. Serve immediately.

If stored in the refrigerator for a few days, the flavor of this sauce won't deteriorate, but the fat will separate out and affect the texture.

Suggested uses

Spoon over chicken breasts, steamed broccoli, or poached eggs.

macronutrient profile (per serving)
2 tbsp (30 ml) per serving

	Grams	Calories	%-Cals
Calories		174	
Fat	17	152	87%
Saturated	10	90	52%
Polyunsaturated	1	8	5%
Monounsaturated	5	46	26%
Carbohydrate	1	5	3%
Dietary Fiber	0		
Protein	4	18	10%

marsala sauce

There's a reason this sauce is so popular. It's rich but not overly heavy, and the flavor is plate-licking good. For even more flavor, if you've just pan-seared a steak, pork chop, or chicken thigh in a pan, then use that same pan with some of the leftover drippings to make this sauce.

Makes 1 cup (250 ml), serves 8
Time in the kitchen: 20 minutes

2 tablespoons (30 ml) extra virgin olive oil or butter

1 shallot, finely chopped

2 cups (500 ml) sliced mushrooms

1 to 2 garlic cloves, finely chopped

½ cup (125 ml) dry marsala wine or white wine

1 cup (250 ml) chicken or beef stock

1 tablespoon (15 ml) whipping cream or coconut milk (optional)

1 tablespoon (15 ml) finely chopped parsley

Sauté the shallot and mushrooms in the oil or butter over medium heat until the liquid has evaporated and mushrooms are lightly browned, about five minutes.

Add garlic, and sauté one minute more.

Turn heat to high. Add the marsala. Boil for three minutes.

Add the stock and simmer five more minutes to reduce some of the liquid.

To thicken, add whipping cream or coconut milk, and simmer a few minutes more. (Or, just add a little butter).

Garnish with parsley.

Suggested uses

Serve over pork chops and steak, or spoon over roasted vegetables.

macronutrient profile (per serving)
2 tbsp (30 ml) per serving

	Grams	Calories	%-Cals
Calories		65	
Fat	5	43	66%
Saturated	1	10	16%
Polyunsaturated	1	5	7%
Monounsaturated	3	27	42%
Carbohydrate	2	8	12%
Dietary Fiber	0		
Protein	4	14	22%

almost traditional turkey gravy

This gravy recipe perfectly mimics flour-thickened gravy made from pan drippings. It's thick, meaty-tasting, and too delicious to save only for Thanksgiving. If you do happen to be roasting a whole bird, then by all means use the pan drippings instead of stock.

Makes 1 cup (250 ml), serves 8
Time in the kitchen: 10 minutes

½ cup (125 ml) coconut milk

1 cup (250 ml) turkey, chicken, or beef stock, or pan juices from roasting a bird

1 tablespoon (15 ml) tapioca starch (also called tapioca flour) mixed with 1 tablespoon (15 ml) cold water

1 teaspoon (5 ml) tamari

¼ teaspoon (1 ml) celery salt

¼ teaspoon (1 ml) poultry seasoning

Heat the coconut milk to gentle boil.

In a separate pot, heat the stock.

Whisk the tapioca mixture into the coconut milk, keeping it at a gentle boil. The milk should thicken immediately and have a smooth, paste-like texture.

Slowly whisk the stock into coconut milk and remove from heat.

Add tamari, celery salt, and poultry seasoning.

Serve immediately.

This gravy can be re-heated, however, if it is returned to heat for too long the starch will break down and the gravy will lose its thickness.

Suggested uses

As a topping for turkey, of course, but also delicious poured over puréed cauliflower and meatballs.

macronutrient profile (per serving)
2 tbsp (30 ml) per serving

	Grams	Calories	%-Cals
Calories		41	
Fat	3	29	72%
Saturated	3	25	61%
Polyunsaturated	0	1	2%
Monounsaturated	0	2	6%
Carbohydrate	2	8	18%
Dietary Fiber	0		
Protein	1	4	10%

roasted meat gravy

This versatile gravy is made from the pan juices of beef, lamb, or pork roasts. You could even make a similar version using the drippings from a single pork chop or steak that's been seared in a saucepan. If you're lucky, the gravy will have savory bits of meat and fat mixed in.

Makes ½ to 1 cup (125 to 250 ml), serves 8
Time in the kitchen: 15 minutes

Pan juices from 3 to 4 pounds (1.5 to 2 kg) of roasted meat

½ cup (125 ml) white wine

1 cup (250 ml) beef stock

1 tablespoon (15 ml) butter

Pour the pan drippings out of the roasting pan and into a small bowl. Skim a little bit of the fat off the top so the sauce isn't too greasy.

Set the roasting pan on the stove over medium heat, add wine, and bring to a boil. Scrape up the browned bits left from the meat so they mix with the wine. Boil until the wine is reduced by half, three to five minutes.

Whisk in pan drippings and stock. Keep at a gentle boil, stirring a few times as the sauce thickens, five minutes.

Add butter.

If you want to thicken the gravy even more, add arrowroot or tapioca starch (page 7).

Suggested uses

Serve with any type of roasted meat, chicken cutlets, or sautéed Portobello mushrooms.

macronutrient profile (per serving)
2 tbsp (30 ml) per serving

	Grams	Calories	%-Cals
Calories		23	
Fat	2	14	59%
Saturated	1	8	34%
Polyunsaturated	0	1	2%
Monounsaturated	0	3	15%
Carbohydrate	1	5	20%
Dietary Fiber	0		
Protein	1	5	22%

sausage gravy

Skip the biscuits and serve this hearty gravy over a plate of eggs. The type of sausage you use obviously affects the flavor of the gravy. Pork sausage is traditional, but I also love to use plain ground lamb instead of sausage and then add a pinch of fresh sage or parsley.

Makes 2 cups (500 ml), serves 8
Time in the kitchen: 20 minutes

1 cup or ½ pound (250 ml or 230 g) ground meat or loose sausage

1 tablespoon (15 ml) smooth, unsalted, raw almond butter

1 cup (250 ml) whole cream or coconut milk

Cook meat in a skillet over medium heat until done.

Remove the sausage from the pan, leaving the fat.

Add the almond butter to the pan, stirring with the rendered fat until smooth.

Slowly add the cream, stirring to combine with the almond butter.

Gently boil the cream until it thickens, three to five minutes.

Add the sausage back to the pan.

Simmer a few minutes then serve.

Suggested uses

Serve with root vegetable hash, slices of fresh tomato with scrambled eggs, or sautéed greens.

macronutrient profile (per serving)

4 tbsp (60 ml) per serving

	Grams	Calories	%-Cals
Calories		90	
Fat	8	73	81%
Saturated	7	60	66%
Polyunsaturated	0	1	1%
Monounsaturated	1	8	9%
Carbohydrate	1	3	3%
Dietary Fiber	0		
Protein	4	14	16%

onion gravy

This gravy is both thickened and flavored by a purée of sweet, caramelized onions. Although especially good over chicken, there's no reason you can't try it with other types of meat, too. And don't forget to pour it over sides like puréed cauliflower and puréed root vegetables.

Makes 2 cups (500 ml), serves 16
Time in the kitchen: 50 minutes

3 tablespoon (45 ml) butter or animal fat

1 large white or yellow onion, thinly sliced

2 ribs of celery, thinly sliced

2 cups (500 ml) chicken stock (page 10)

In a large saucepan or deep pot, melt butter or animal fat over medium heat.

Add the onion and celery and cover with a lid. Cook for thirty minutes, stirring a few times to make sure the onions aren't burning. Turn the heat down to medium-low to prevent this if necessary.

Transfer the onion and celery to a blender and purée until as smooth as possible. Add a little stock if it makes blending easier.

Heat the stock over medium-high and whisk in the onion purée.

Gently boil for five minutes.

Add salt and pepper to taste.

If you want to thicken the gravy even more, add arrowroot or tapioca starch (page 7).

Suggested uses

Serve with roasted chicken, pot roast, and pork chops.

macronutrient profile (per serving)
2 tbsp (30 ml) per serving

	Grams	Calories	%-Cals
Calories		35	
Fat	3	23	66%
Saturated	2	14	39%
Polyunsaturated	0	1	3%
Monounsaturated	1	7	19%
Carbohydrate	2	8	24%
Dietary Fiber	0		
Protein	1	4	11%

onion-mushroom sauce

A surprisingly meaty-tasting sauce that's actually flavored with just mushrooms and onions. Just as good over salmon as it is over steak.

Makes 1 ½ cups (375 ml), serves 12
Time in the kitchen: 30 minutes

2 tablespoons (30 ml) butter

2 tablespoons (30 ml) extra virgin olive oil

1 white or yellow onion, chopped

1 cup (250 ml) sliced mushrooms

1 teaspoon (5 ml) balsamic vinegar

2 cups (500 ml) beef stock

Over medium heat, melt the butter and olive oil in a large saucepan.

Add the onion and mushrooms and cover with a lid. Cook for ten minutes, until onions and mushrooms are soft—you don't want them to burn, so if needed turn the heat down slightly.

Add the vinegar and put the lid back on for five minutes. Stir once or twice.

Add the stock. If the heat has been turned down, then bring it back up to medium. Simmer for ten minutes without a cover.

Serve as is, or add a thickener (page 7).

Suggested uses

Spoon over burger patties, pork loin, and chicken thighs.

macronutrient profile (per serving)
2 tbsp (30 ml) per serving

	Grams	Calories	%-Cals
Calories		51	
Fat	4	38	76%
Saturated	2	14	28%
Polyunsaturated	0	3	6%
Monounsaturated	2	20	39%
Carbohydrate	2	8	15%
Dietary Fiber	0		
Protein	1	5	9%

quick mushroom sauce

This is exactly the type of sauce you should make if you're browning meat in a pan on the stove. Once the cooked meat is out of the pan, use the remaining fat to sauté the mushrooms and shallot and you're well on your way to a delicious sauce.

Makes 1 cup (250 ml), serves 8
Time in the kitchen: 20 minutes

2 tablespoons (30 ml) fat (such as animal fat, extra virgin olive oil, coconut oil)

8 ounces (227 g) cremini mushrooms, sliced

1 large shallot, finely chopped

¾ cup (175 ml) chicken or beef stock

1 tablespoon (15 ml) butter

1 tablespoon (15 ml) finely chopped fresh herb (such as chives, parsley, basil or thyme) (optional)

Heat fat over medium-high heat in a large skillet.

Add mushrooms and shallot. Sauté until soft and golden, about seven minutes.

Stir occasionally, but not too much or the mushrooms won't brown properly.

Add stock. Boil for five minutes.

Remove from heat. Stir in butter and fresh herbs.

Suggested uses

Pour over baked salmon, and use it to dress up steaks and pork chops.

macronutrient profile (per serving)
2 tbsp (30 ml) per serving

	Grams	Calories	%-Cals
Calories		62	
Fat	5	46	75%
Saturated	2	14	22%
Polyunsaturated	1	5	7%
Monounsaturated	3	27	44%
Carbohydrate	3	10	16%
Dietary Fiber	0		
Protein	1	6	9%

slow simmered mushroom sauce

This vegetarian sauce also has a surprisingly rich and meaty flavor. It could be either the Portobello mushrooms or the long simmering time that gives it this ragu-like quality. This recipe involves a lot of fine chopping, but it's necessary for the flavor of the dish. Larger chunks won't meld together as well. If you like, use a food processor to grate the onions and carrots instead of chopping them by hand.

Makes 3 cups (750 ml), serves 12
Time in the kitchen: 1 hour, plus 1 ½ hours to simmer

1 ounce (28 g) dried mushrooms

¼ cup (60 ml) extra virgin olive oil or unsalted butter

2 yellow onions, finely chopped

2 carrots, finely chopped or grated

2 celery ribs, finely chopped

4 garlic cloves, finely chopped

½ cup (125 ml) finely chopped fresh parsley

½ teaspoon (2 ml) dried dill

1 teaspoon (5 ml) dried oregano

2 Portobello mushrooms, finely chopped

¼ teaspoon (1 ml) salt

¼ teaspoon (1 ml) black pepper

½ cup (125 ml) red wine

2 tablespoons (30 ml) tomato paste

Soak dried mushrooms in a bowl with 2 cups (500 ml) hot water. Set aside.

Heat olive oil or butter in a deep pot over medium heat.

Add the onions and cook thirty-five minutes, stirring occasionally, until onions are soft and golden. If they begin to burn around the edges, turn the heat down slightly.

Add the carrots and celery and sauté ten more minutes.

Add the garlic, parsley, dill, and oregano.

Remove the dried mushrooms from the water they are soaking in, reserving the water in the bowl. Dried mushrooms often leave some grit behind; you can strain it out by pouring the water through a coffee filter or fine mesh sieve.

Chop the re-hydrated mushrooms up and add them to the cooking pot along with the Portobello mushrooms, salt, and pepper.

cont'd »

Turn the heat up to high. Add the red wine and simmer for five minutes.

Whisk the tomato paste with 1 cup (250 ml) of the mushroom water. Add the liquid to the pot.

Once the sauce comes back to a simmer, turn the heat down to just a notch above low.

Cover the pot and simmer for one and a half hours, stirring occasionally.

Add additional salt and pepper to taste if needed before serving.

Suggested uses

A topping for spaghetti squash, a bowl of puréed sweet potatoes or a thick pork chop.

macronutrient profile (per serving)
4 tbsp (60 ml) per serving

	Grams	Calories	%-Cals
Calories		76	
Fat	5	42	55%
Saturated	1	6	8%
Polyunsaturated	1	5	6%
Monounsaturated	3	30	39%
Carbohydrate	7	29	38%
Dietary Fiber	2		
Protein	1	5	7%

bolognese sauce

When you have a Bolognese sauce this good, who needs noodles? Although pre-ground meat is convenient, consider grinding your own. The flavor and freshness can't be beat.

Makes 3 to 4 cups (700 to 950 ml), serves 16
Time in the kitchen: 1 hour, plus 3 hours to simmer

¼ cup (60 ml) extra virgin olive oil

2 tablespoons (30 ml) unsalted butter

1 rib of celery, finely chopped

½ medium-sized yellow or white onion, finely chopped

1 carrot, finely chopped

2 garlic cloves, finely chopped

1 pound ground beef (450 g) (buy chuck and grind your own)

1 pound ground pork (450 g) (buy shoulder and grind your own)

1 teaspoon (5 ml) dried oregano

2 tablespoons (30 ml) tomato paste

½ cup (125 ml) red wine

1 28-ounce can (794 g) whole peeled tomatoes (with juice)

If you don't want to cut the celery, onion, carrot, and garlic by hand, pulse them in a food processor until finely chopped.

Heat the oil and butter in a large pot over medium heat.

Add the celery, onions, carrots, and garlic. Cook, stirring frequently, until soft and lightly browned, about fifteen minutes. Add salt and pepper.

Reduce the heat to low and put a lid on the pot, stirring occasionally as the veggies cook another ten minutes until really soft and caramelized.

Add the beef, pork, and oregano. Break up the meat as it cooks and browns, about ten minutes. Lightly salt the meat.

Stir in the tomato paste and cook a few minutes.

Add the wine and simmer, stirring, until the wine mostly evaporates, about five minutes.

cont'd »

Put the tomatoes and their juice in a large bowl and break them up with your hands. Add the tomatoes to the cooking pot.

Reduce heat to low and simmer uncovered, stirring occasionally, until sauce is very, thick, about three hours. Liberally salt to taste as the sauce cooks.

Suggested uses

A sauce for strips of sautéed zucchini, roasted spaghetti squash, and steamed, grated cauliflower.

macronutrient profile (per serving)

4 tbsp (60 ml) per serving

	Grams	Calories	%-Cals
Calories		177	
Fat	12	111	63%
Saturated	4	38	22%
Polyunsaturated	1	10	5%
Monounsaturated	6	55	31%
Carbohydrate	5	19	11%
Dietary Fiber	1		
Protein	12	46	26%

marinara sauce

This rich marinara sauce, similar to a popular one by Italian cookbook author Marcella Hazan, turns out perfectly every time. Just make sure to use high-quality canned tomatoes. Pour over spaghetti squash or thinly sliced, sautéed zucchini or use it as a topping for chicken or steak.

Makes 2 cups (500 ml), serves 16
Time in the kitchen: 1 hour

1 28-ounce can (794 g) whole tomatoes (with juice)

5 tablespoons (75 ml) butter

5 garlic cloves, thinly sliced

1 teaspoon (5 ml) dried oregano

1 yellow onion, peeled and cut in half

¼ cup (60 ml) finely chopped fresh basil

Season to taste with salt

Pour the tomatoes into a large bowl and use your hands to break them up.

In a deep saucepan or pot over medium heat, melt the butter with the garlic.

When the butter has melted, add the tomatoes, oregano, and onion halves. Bring to a simmer.

Simmer uncovered over medium to medium-low heat. The sauce should bubble gently the whole time, but not reach a full-on boil. Stir occasionally.

After forty-five minutes, turn off the heat, remove the onion (you can eat it, it's really tasty) and add the basil.

Season to taste with salt.

Suggested uses

Mix with ground meat, strips of steak, or grilled eggplant.

macronutrient profile (per serving)
2 tbsp (30 ml) per serving

	Grams	Calories	%-Cals
Calories		53	
Fat	4	33	62%
Saturated	2	21	39%
Polyunsaturated	0	2	3%
Monounsaturated	1	8	16%
Carbohydrate	4	18	33%
Dietary Fiber	1		
Protein	1	3	5%

pancetta tomato sauce

This vibrant tomato sauce is only cooked long enough for the tomatoes to release their juice. Pancetta (or bacon) adds richness to this fresh, chunky sauce that's fantastic spooned over eggs, especially with a few strips of steak on the side.

Makes 3 cups (750 ml), serves 12
Time in the kitchen: 25 minutes

⅓ to ½ pound (150 to 225 g) pancetta or bacon, cut into small pieces

½ cup (125 ml) white wine

4 to 6 fresh tomatoes, chopped

3 scallions, chopped

Season to taste with salt

Over medium heat, brown pancetta or bacon until cooked.

Turn heat up to medium-high and add wine. Gentle boil for about three minutes to reduce liquid by half.

Add fresh tomatoes and their juice. Keep at a gentle boil for five minutes.

Top with scallions.

Suggested uses

A sauce for halibut, scallops, and steak.

macronutrient profile (per serving)
4 tbsp (60 ml) per serving

	Grams	Calories	%-Cals
Calories		104	
Fat	9	78	75%
Saturated	3	26	25%
Polyunsaturated	1	9	9%
Monounsaturated	4	35	33%
Carbohydrate	4	14	14%
Dietary Fiber	1		
Protein	3	12	11%

peppery roasted tomato sauce

There's no need to wait until summer to make this tomato sauce. It's fairly easy to find sweet cherry tomatoes year round, plus, roasting them concentrates the flavor. Sichuan peppercorns have a distinct, lemony flavor, but if you can't find them, simply double the amount of regular peppercorns. Spoon this sauce liberally over seafood or red meat.

Makes 3 cups (750 ml), serves 12
Time in the kitchen: 45 minutes

1 pound (500 g) cherry tomatoes

¼ cup (60 ml) extra virgin olive oil

4 cloves of garlic, finely chopped or pressed

½ teaspoon (2 ml) whole peppercorns (black, white, green, or a blend of all three)

½ teaspoon (2 ml) whole Sichuan peppercorns

Season to taste with salt

Preheat oven to 400 °F (200 °C).

In a rimmed baking sheet, combine tomatoes, olive oil, and garlic. Roast forty minutes, stirring occasionally, until the tomatoes are soft and many have split open.

While the tomatoes roast, heat a frying pan over medium-high heat. Add peppercorns and toast for one to two minutes, shaking the pan once or twice, until the peppercorns start releasing their aroma.

Chop the peppercorns finely with a knife, or put the peppercorns between two sheets of parchment paper or in a sealed plastic bag and crush them with a rolling pin.

Remove the tomatoes from the oven. Sprinkle pepper on top. Add sea salt to taste.

Suggested uses

Serve alongside grilled salmon, shrimp, or beef kabobs.

macronutrient profile (per serving)
4 tbsp (60 ml) per serving

	Grams	Calories	%-Cals
Calories		51	
Fat	5	41	82%
Saturated	1	6	12%
Polyunsaturated	1	5	9%
Monounsaturated	3	30	59%
Carbohydrate	2	8	15%
Dietary Fiber	1		
Protein	0	2	3%

veracruz sauce

This popular sauce from Mexico is traditionally served with white fish. The pickled jalapeños, capers and green olives give the sauce a unique flavor and briny bite. Whole tomatoes in a can always seem to have better flavor and texture than canned diced tomatoes. The easiest way to break the whole tomatoes up is to pour them in a large bowl and use your hands to squeeze the tomatoes into tiny pieces.

Makes 2 to 3 cups (500 to 750 ml),
serves 12
Time in the kitchen: 1 hour

1 to 2 tablespoons (30 ml) extra virgin olive oil

1 white or yellow onion, coarsely chopped

4 garlic cloves, finely chopped

1 28-ounce (794 g) can whole tomatoes in juice

1 cup (250 ml) pitted green olives

1 tablespoon (15 ml) capers

2 pickled jalapeño peppers, chopped or 2 tablespoons (30 ml) canned diced green chiles

1 teaspoon (5 ml) ground cumin

¼ cup (60 ml) coarsely chopped parsley

1 teaspoon (5 ml) dried oregano

1 bay leaf

Season to taste with salt

Suggested uses

On top of white fish, over roasted cauliflower, and as a filling for omelets.

Heat oil in a deep pot or saucepan over medium-low heat.

Add onions and cook until golden, about ten minutes.

Stir in garlic, and cook for one minute.

Break up the canned tomatoes with your hands then add to the pot with the juice. Simmer tomatoes over medium heat for ten minutes without a lid.

Add olives, capers, jalapeños, cumin, parsley, oregano, and bay leaf.

Simmer uncovered for twenty minutes.

Season to taste with salt.

macronutrient profile (per serving)
4 tbsp (60 ml) per serving

	Grams	Calories	%-Cals
Calories		79	
Fat	5	48	61%
Saturated	1	7	9%
Polyunsaturated	1	5	7%
Monounsaturated	4	35	43%
Carbohydrate	7	27	34%
Dietary Fiber	2		
Protein	1	4	5%

spicy poblano sauce

*The spiciness of poblano peppers varies, so you never know how smokin'
hot this sauce might be. The whole cream or coconut milk mellows the
heat, though, so even those with a low tolerance for spicy food will love
the sauce.*

Makes 1 cup (250 ml), serves 8
Time in the kitchen: 45 minutes

4 poblano chiles

2 tablespoons (30 ml) unsalted
butter

1 shallot, finely chopped

½ cup (125 ml) chicken stock
(page 10)

½ cup (125 ml) heavy cream or
coconut milk

Season to taste with salt

To roast the peppers, set them directly
over a gas flame, grill flame, or under a
broiler. Roast, turning with tongs, until
blackened all over. Put peppers into a
bowl covered with plastic wrap or in a
sealed plastic bag to steam the skin off.
Let stand ten minutes then rub the black
skin off and remove the stem and inner
seeds. Coarsely chop the peppers.

Melt the butter in a pan over medium heat.

Add the shallot and sauté a few minutes.

Add the peppers and chicken stock.
Bring the stock to a boil and simmer five
minutes.

Pour into a food processor or blender.
Purée until very smooth.

Return to the pan and add cream. Simmer
on low until sauce is warm. Season to
taste with salt.

macronutrient profile (per serving)
2 tbsp (30 ml) per serving

	Grams	Calories	%-Cals
Calories		77	
Fat	6	56	73%
Saturated	5	42	54%
Polyunsaturated	0	2	3%
Monounsaturated	1	9	12%
Carbohydrate	3	12	16%
Dietary Fiber	0		
Protein	2	9	12%

Suggested uses

Pour over chicken and steak, or use
the sauce as a creamy topping or hot
dip for vegetables.

bell pepper sauce

Every home cook should have their own version of creole sauce, and this is mine. Bell peppers dominate and lend a sweet flavor. Spoon over just about anything.

Makes 2 to 3 cups (500 to 750 ml), serves 12
Time in the kitchen: 1 hour

2 tablespoons (30 ml) extra virgin olive oil or other fat

1 onion, finely chopped

2 garlic cloves, finely chopped

1 green bell pepper, finely chopped

1 red bell pepper finely chopped

1 yellow or orange bell pepper, finely chopped

1 teaspoon (5 ml) paprika

¼ teaspoon (1 ml) black pepper

½ teaspoon (2 ml) dried oregano

½ teaspoon (2 ml) dried thyme

½ teaspoon (2 ml) onion powder

2 tomatoes, coarsely chopped

1 tablespoon (15 ml) tomato paste

1 cup (250 ml) chicken stock (page 10)

2 to 3 green onions, chopped

Season to taste with salt

Suggested uses

Serve with grilled sausage, fried eggs, or pork chops.

Warm olive oil in a large pot over medium heat.

Add onion and sauté ten minutes, until soft.

Add garlic and peppers and sauté ten minutes more, stirring frequently.

Add spices and tomatoes.

Whisk tomato paste with chicken broth in a small bowl. Pour the broth into the pot and boil uncovered on high until sauce reaches desired consistency, five to ten minutes.

Add green onions and salt to taste.

macronutrient profile (per serving)
4 tbsp (60 ml) per serving

	Grams	Calories	%-Cals
Calories		60	
Fat	3	26	44%
Saturated	1	5	7%
Polyunsaturated	0	4	6%
Monounsaturated	2	17	27%
Carbohydrate	6	23	38%
Dietary Fiber	1		
Protein	3	11	18%

roasted red pepper pesto

You can buy roasted red peppers, but they taste so much better when you roast them yourself. Using the right kind of paprika also makes a big difference in the flavor of this sweet, smoky pesto. Spanish sweet smoked paprika has a different flavor than Hungarian paprika and much more flavor than generic paprika.

Makes 1 cup (250 ml), serves 8
Time in the kitchen: 20 minutes

2 red bell peppers, roasted

½ cup (125 ml) walnuts or macadamia nuts

1 to 2 garlic cloves, thinly sliced

2 teaspoons (10 ml) sherry vinegar

¼ cup (60 ml) extra virgin olive oil

½ teaspoon (2 ml) sweet smoked paprika

Season to taste with salt

To roast the peppers, place directly over a gas flame, grill flame or under a broiler. Roast, turning with tongs, until blackened all over. Put peppers into a bowl covered with plastic wrap or in a sealed plastic bag to steam the skin off. Let stand ten minutes then rub the black skin off and remove the inner seeds and stem.

In a food processor, blend nuts and garlic until nuts are very finely chopped.

Add remaining ingredients, including the roasted peppers, and blend until smooth.

Season to taste with salt. The flavor of this sauce gets even better after refrigerating the sauce overnight.

Suggested uses

A topping for skirt steak and grilled eggplant, or tossed with arugula as a thick salad dressing.

macronutrient profile (per serving)
2 tbsp (30 ml) per serving

	Grams	Calories	%-Cals
Calories		126	
Fat	12	105	83%
Saturated	1	12	10%
Polyunsaturated	4	38	30%
Monounsaturated	6	51	40%
Carbohydrate	4	15	12%
Dietary Fiber	1		
Protein	2	7	5%

coconut-cilantro pesto

Tangy and slightly sweet with the herbaceous, floral flavor of cilantro, this creamy pesto is a favorite on everything from fish to pork.

Makes 1 cup (250 ml), serves 8
Time in the kitchen: 10 minutes

2 heaping cups (500 ml) or large handfuls of cilantro, stems mostly cut off

¼ teaspoon (1 ml) ground cumin

2 tablespoons (30 ml) unsalted, smooth, raw almond butter

Juice of ½ lime

¼ cup (60 ml) coconut milk

¼ teaspoon (1 ml) salt

Blend all ingredients in a food processor until very smooth.

Add more coconut milk if needed to thin out the pesto.

Suggested uses

Serve with pork loin, grilled steak, and shrimp.

macronutrient profile (per serving)
2 tbsp (30 ml) per serving

	Grams	Calories	%-Cals
Calories		44	
Fat	4	34	77%
Saturated	2	14	31%
Polyunsaturated	1	6	13%
Monounsaturated	1	12	28%
Carbohydrate	1	6	13%
Dietary Fiber	1		
Protein	1	5	10%

arugula-watercress pesto

This nutrient-rich pesto has a peppery kick from both the arugula and watercress. If you can't find watercress at your market, simply double the amount of arugula. You can make this pesto the traditional way with grated Parmigiano-Reggiano cheese, or go dairy-free by using avocado to give the pesto a creamy texture.

Makes 1 cup (250 ml), serves 8
Time in the kitchen: 10 minutes

¼ cup (60 ml) walnuts or other nut (such as macadamia)

1 to 2 garlic cloves, thinly sliced

1 cup (250 ml) grated Parmigiano-Reggiano cheese or half an avocado

1 cup (250 ml) arugula

1 bunch of watercress, stems cut off

½ cup (125 ml) extra virgin olive oil

Blend nuts, garlic, and cheese or avocado until nuts are finely chopped.

Add the greens and pulse a few times, then with the blade still running slowly pour in the olive oil.

Blend until pesto reaches desired consistency. Add salt to taste.

Suggested uses

Toss with chunks of chicken, dollop on salmon, and stir into scrambled eggs.

macronutrient profile (per serving)
2 tbsp (30 ml) per serving

	Grams	Calories	%-Cals
Calories		204	
Fat	20	176	86%
Saturated	4	38	19%
Polyunsaturated	3	29	14%
Monounsaturated	11	101	50%
Carbohydrate	1	6	3%
Dietary Fiber	0		
Protein	6	23	11%

creamy arugula sauce

A bright-green peppery sauce with a fresh, almost grassy flavor. Fantastic over seafood.

Makes 1 cup (250 ml), serves 8
Time in the kitchen: 10 minutes

3 large handfuls of arugula

¾ cup (175 ml) sour cream, or full-fat Greek yogurt

¼ cup (60 ml) fresh parsley leaves

Season to taste with salt

Purée all the ingredients in a blender until smooth. Serve cold.

Suggested uses

Drizzle over halibut and cod, or take it in a different direction with lamb chops.

macronutrient profile (per serving)

2 tbsp (30 ml) per serving

	Grams	Calories	%-Cals
Calories		44	
Fat	4	38	86%
Saturated	3	23	51%
Polyunsaturated	0	2	5%
Monounsaturated	1	10	23%
Carbohydrate	1	4	8%
Dietary Fiber	0		
Protein	1	3	6%

minty caper sauce

Admittedly, this piquant sauce walks a very fine line between sauce and dressing, but it's so good over meat and fish that it ended up in the sauce chapter. Don't let this stop you from pouring it over salads, although it's even better on top of roasted and grilled vegetables. If you're not a fan of mint, use fresh dill instead.

Makes ½ cup (125 ml), serves 4
Time in the kitchen: 5 minutes

¼ cup (60 ml) capers, drained

1 tablespoon (15 ml) chopped mint

¼ cup (60 ml) extra virgin olive oil

2 tablespoons (30 ml) lemon juice

Season to taste with salt

Put all ingredients together in a sealed container and shake to blend well.

Add salt to taste if needed; ¼ teaspoon (1 ml) or less of salt is usually about right.

Suggested uses

A perfect sauce for lamb chops, grilled zucchini, and any type of white fish.

macronutrient profile (per serving)
2 tbsp (30 ml) per serving

	Grams	Calories	%-Cals
Calories		127	
Fat	14	122	96%
Saturated	2	18	14%
Polyunsaturated	2	20	16%
Monounsaturated	10	88	69%
Carbohydrate	1	4	3%
Dietary Fiber	1		
Protein	0	1	1%

fennel-olive tapenade

Usually olives are the main ingredient in tapenade. In this recipe, Kalamatas are blended with fennel, giving the tapenade a mellow anise flavor. It's not the prettiest sauce you'll ever see, but the stunning flavor makes up for the lack of vibrant color.

Makes 1 cup (250 ml), serves 8
Time in the kitchen: 25 minutes

¼ cup (60 ml) extra virgin olive oil

2 small fennel bulbs, thinly sliced (outer layer of the bulb and green fronds removed)

½ white or yellow onion, thinly sliced

½ cup (125 ml) pitted Kalamata olives

Season to taste with salt

Heat olive oil in a saucepan over medium-high heat. Add fennel and onion and sauté until soft, twelve to fifteen minutes.

Scrape fennel, onion, and any oil left in the pan into a food processor.

Add olives and blend the mixture until desired consistency is reached.

Add salt to taste.

The tapenade can be served at room temperature or gently heated before serving.

Suggested uses

Dollop on a pork chop, salmon fillet, or tomatoes and mozzarella.

macronutrient profile (per serving)
2 tbsp (30 ml) per serving

	Grams	Calories	%-Cals
Calories		90	
Fat	7	65	73%
Saturated	1	9	10%
Polyunsaturated	1	7	8%
Monounsaturated	5	47	53%
Carbohydrate	5	21	23%
Dietary Fiber	2		
Protein	1	4	4%

leek-garlic sauce

*It's a mystery why leeks are less popular than onions. Their mild, buttery
flavor is fantastic with just about anything. I like to either spread this
thick sauce on a plate and lay a fillet of salmon or halibut on top, or thin
the sauce out with whole cream and drizzle it on chicken.*

Makes ½ to 1 cup (125 to 250 ml),
serves 8
Time in the kitchen: 35 minutes

¼ cup (60 ml) unsalted butter

4 garlic cloves, thinly sliced

4 leeks (dark green part cut off) cut
into ¼-inch-thick (6 mm) slices

1 tablespoon (15 ml) water

Chicken stock (page 10), cream,
or coconut milk to thin sauce
(optional)

Melt butter in pot over medium-low
heat.

Add garlic and sauté three minutes.

Add leeks and sauté one or two minutes
more, then add water and cover pot.

Reduce heat to low. Cook until leeks
are tender, stirring often, about twenty
minutes.

Purée in a food processor until smooth.
If desired, add as much stock, cream,
or coconut milk as you like to thin the
sauce out.

Suggested uses

A sauce for roasted chicken and pork
chops, or a topping for puréed root
vegetables.

macronutrient profile (per serving)
2 tbsp (30 ml) per serving

	Grams	Calories	%-Cals
Calories		85	
Fat	6	54	64%
Saturated	4	33	38%
Polyunsaturated	0	2	3%
Monounsaturated	2	14	16%
Carbohydrate	7	28	32%
Dietary Fiber	1		
Protein	1	4	4%

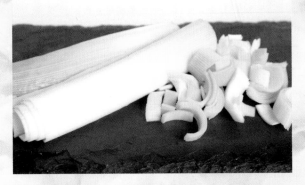

coconut-shallot sauce

This rich, creamy sauce has a naturally sweet flavor from the coconut milk and sautéed shallot. Mild, white fish soaks the flavor right up, or you can pour the sauce over sautéed greens for a quick version of creamed spinach or kale.

Makes ½ cup (125 ml), serves 4
Time in the kitchen: 20 minutes

1 tablespoon (15 ml) extra virgin olive oil

3 tablespoon (45 ml) unsalted butter

1 small shallot, thinly sliced

Juice of ½ small lemon

½ cup (125 ml) coconut milk

Warm olive oil and butter in a skillet over medium heat.

Add shallot. Sauté three minutes.

Add lemon juice and sauté one minute more then add coconut milk.

Bring to a gentle boil for five minutes, stirring as the sauce thickens.

Suggested uses

Drizzle over cod, shrimp, or pork cutlets.

macronutrient profile (per serving)
2 tbsp (30 ml) per serving

	Grams	Calories	%-Cals
Calories		172	
Fat	18	162	94%
Saturated	11	101	59%
Polyunsaturated	1	7	4%
Monounsaturated	5	45	26%
Carbohydrate	2	7	4%
Dietary Fiber	0		
Protein	1	3	2%

lemon butter sauce

It doesn't get any easier than this. The richness of the butter is cut by the lemon's acidity, creating the perfect balance of flavor. You can also add capers or fresh herbs to this sauce. It's especially good over any type of seafood but can also be drizzled on cooked veggies.

Makes ¼ cup (60 ml), serves 2
Time in the kitchen: 5 minutes

5 tablespoons (75 ml) unsalted butter

1 teaspoon (5 ml) Dijon mustard (page 172)

Juice of ½ lemon

Melt butter in a saucepan over medium heat. Within a few minutes, the butter will get foamy then start to turn golden brown. You can take the butter off early, before it browns, or let it brown until it has a rich, nutty flavor.

Pour the butter in a bowl. Whisk in mustard and lemon juice. Serve immediately.

Suggested uses

Drizzle over halibut, salmon, and sautéed spinach.

macronutrient profile (per serving)

2 tbsp (30 ml) per serving

	Grams	Calories	%-Cals
Calories		267	
Fat	29	261	98%
Saturated	18	162	61%
Polyunsaturated	1	9	3%
Monounsaturated	8	68	25%
Carbohydrate	1	4	1%
Dietary Fiber	0		
Protein	1	2	1%

brown butter-sage sauce

Even if you never use sage for anything else in the kitchen, buy it for this amazing combination. When fried in butter, the pungent flavor of sage mellows and the leaves become so paper-thin that they melt in your mouth. Traditionally tossed with pasta, I prefer to serve butter and sage with spaghetti squash, thin strips of sautéed zucchini, or fish.

Makes ¼ to ½ cup (60 to 125 ml), serves 4
Time in the kitchen: 10 minutes

5 tablespoons (75 ml) unsalted butter

20 to 30 fresh sage leaves

Pinch of sea salt

In a saucepan over medium heat, melt butter.

Just as soon as it melts, add sage leaves.

After about three minutes the leaves will start getting crispy and you will smell the nutty aroma of the butter browning. When the leaves are crispy and the butter is golden brown, turn off the heat.

Sprinkle the leaves lightly with sea salt and pour the butter and sage directly onto whatever you're serving.

Suggested uses

Delicious on everything from pan-seared white fish to pork to roasted sweet potatoes.

macronutrient profile (per serving)
2 tbsp (30 ml) per serving

	Grams	Calories	%-Cals
Calories		163	
Fat	16	140	86%
Saturated	10	88	54%
Polyunsaturated	1	7	4%
Monounsaturated	4	36	22%
Carbohydrate	5	19	12%
Dietary Fiber	3		
Protein	1	4	2%

tomato-coconut curry sauce

This simple, gently spiced sauce isn't a traditional curry. It is, however, the perfect quick curry sauce when time is tight. You can also turn this sauce into the base for soup by adding a cup or two of chicken stock (page 10). As either a sauce or soup, it's fantastic with seafood, chicken, and red meat.

Makes 2 cups (500 ml), serves 8
Time in the kitchen: 35 minutes

2 tablespoons (30 ml) coconut oil, butter, or extra virgin olive oil

½ large white or yellow onion, finely chopped

2 garlic cloves, finely chopped

1 to 2 teaspoons (5 to 10 ml) curry powder

1 ½ teaspoons (7.5 ml) ground cumin

½ teaspoon (2 ml) ground coriander

2 large tomatoes, coarsely chopped

1 cup (250 ml) coconut milk

Cilantro or parsley to garnish

Season to taste with salt

Suggested uses

Simmer with chunks of pork or beef, spoon over a bowl of steamed, grated cauliflower.

Heat oil in a sauté pan over medium-low heat.

Add the onions and cook until soft but not browned, about ten minutes.

Add the garlic and spices and sauté a few minutes more.

Add the tomatoes and coconut milk. Raise heat to medium-high and boil for ten minutes, stirring frequently.

Purée in the blender until smooth.

Add salt to taste.

macronutrient profile (per serving)
4 tbsp (60 ml) per serving

	Grams	Calories	%-Cals
Calories		110	
Fat	10	88	80%
Saturated	8	75	69%
Polyunsaturated	0	2	2%
Monounsaturated	1	6	5%
Carbohydrate	4	17	15%
Dietary Fiber	1		
Protein	1	5	5%

stir-fry sauce

Tart, tangy, salty, sweet, toasty...every flavor in this exciting sauce fights to dominate over the other. Use half to stir-fry meat or vegetables and save the rest to use as a sauce once the meal is cooked. This versatile sauce can also be used as a salad dressing or marinade.

Makes 1 cup (250 ml), serves 8
Time in the kitchen: 10 minutes

½ cup (125 ml) tamari

2 tablespoons (30 ml) unseasoned rice vinegar

Juice of 1 lime

2 tablespoons (30 ml) toasted sesame oil

1 tablespoon (15 ml) raw honey

2 garlic cloves, finely chopped

2 green onions, chopped

Whisk together all ingredients in a small bowl, or combine in a jar or other sealed container and shake until blended.

Suggested uses

Sauté with skirt steak, spoon over ground pork, and toss with cabbage and strips of chicken.

macronutrient profile (per serving)
2 tbsp (30 ml) per serving

	Grams	Calories	%-Cals
Calories		56	
Fat	4	32	57%
Saturated	1	5	8%
Polyunsaturated	1	12	22%
Monounsaturated	1	12	22%
Carbohydrate	4	16	29%
Dietary Fiber	0		
Protein	2	8	14%

tomato salsa

Spicy and just a little bit smoky from the charred tomatoes, this amazing salsa is so much fresher than most anything you can buy in a store. Use it as a dip for veggies, or serve with meat or eggs.

Makes 1 cup (250 ml), serves 8
Time in the kitchen: 25 minutes

1 jalapeño pepper

2 garlic cloves, unpeeled

2 large or 4 smaller tomatoes

¼ teaspoon (1 ml) salt

½ cup (125 ml) finely chopped white or yellow onion

2 tablespoons (30 ml) coarsely chopped cilantro

Juice of 1 lime

Roast the jalapeño and garlic in a dry, heavy skillet over medium heat, about fifteen minutes, turning occasionally and pressing down with a spatula so they blacken and blister on all sides. Cut the stem off the jalapeño and peel the garlic.

Place the tomatoes on a rimmed baking sheet several inches under an oven broiler on high. Roast until the tomato skin blackens and peels back, about five minutes on each side. Let the tomatoes cool.

Peel the tomato skin off over a bowl, reserving the juice and discarding the skin. Peel the garlic cloves.

In a food processor, pulse the jalapeño pepper, garlic, salt, and onion just until blended. Add the tomatoes and pulse a few times until you reach your desired salsa texture. If needed, add the reserved juice from the tomatoes to thin it out.

Add cilantro and lime juice to taste. The flavor of the salsa intensifies if you make it a few hours before serving.

Suggested uses

Use it to add some heat to grilled steak, turkey burgers, and eggs with avocado.

macronutrient profile (per serving)
2 tbsp (30 ml) per serving

	Grams	Calories	%-Cals
Calories		18	
Fat	0	1	6%
Saturated	0	0	1%
Polyunsaturated	0	0	3%
Monounsaturated	0	0	1%
Carbohydrate	4	14	79%
Dietary Fiber	1		
Protein	1	3	14%

carrot salsa

Not at all traditional, but an amazing twist best made with earthy, full-flavored farmers market carrots. Serve alongside any type of protein.

Makes 2 cups (500 ml), serves 8
Time in the kitchen: 10 minutes

2 cups (500 ml) grated carrots

2 tablespoons (30 ml) finely chopped red onion

1 jalapeño pepper, seeded and finely chopped

Small handful of parsley or cilantro leaves, coarsely chopped

2 tablespoons (30 ml) lime juice

1 tablespoon (15 ml) extra virgin olive oil

½ teaspoon (2 ml) ground cumin

¼ teaspoon (1 ml) coriander

¼ teaspoon (1 ml) salt

Toss carrots, onion, jalapeño, and parsley or cilantro in a bowl together.

In a small bowl, whisk together lime juice, olive oil, cumin, coriander, and salt.

Pour dressing over carrot mixture. Mix well.

Suggested uses

A garnish for salmon, pork, and lamb chops.

macronutrient profile (per serving)
4 tbsp (60 ml) per serving

	Grams	Calories	%-Cals
Calories		31	
Fat	2	16	51%
Saturated	0	2	7%
Polyunsaturated	0	2	7%
Monounsaturated	1	11	37%
Carbohydrate	3	14	44%
Dietary Fiber	1		
Protein	0	2	5%

avocado salsa

If you love salsa and guacamole, this green salsa is the best of both worlds. Tomatillos have a tangy flavor that goes perfectly with avocados. You don't need chips to enjoy this salsa; instead, spoon it over grilled steak, chicken, or shrimp.

Makes 2 cups (500 ml), serves 16
Time in the kitchen: 10 minutes

2 ripe avocados, peeled and pitted

2 garlic cloves

5 tomatillos, husked, rinsed, and coarsely chopped

Small handful of cilantro leaves

½ white or yellow onion, coarsely chopped

1 jalapeño pepper, seeded and coarsely chopped

Juice of 1 lime

Season to taste with salt

In a food processor, combine avocados, garlic, tomatillos, cilantro, onion, and jalapeño.

Process until desired consistency is reached, either a chunky or smooth salsa.

Flavor with lime juice and salt.

Suggested uses

Serve with shrimp and red pepper skewers, grilled flank steak, or pork cutlets sautéed with onions.

macronutrient profile (per serving)
2 tbsp (30 ml) per serving

	Grams	Calories	%-Cals
Calories		38	
Fat	3	25	65%
Saturated	0	3	9%
Polyunsaturated	0	3	9%
Monounsaturated	2	15	40%
Carbohydrate	3	11	30%
Dietary Fiber	1		
Protein	1	2	5%

coconut milk whipped cream

You can always make whipped cream by whisking whole cream and vanilla together, but if dairy isn't your thing (or even if it is) you must try this version made with coconut milk. Slightly looser than regular whipped cream, but just as decadent with a naturally sweet, coconut flavor. For extra flavor, finish the whipped cream with a sprinkle of cinnamon.

Makes ½ to 1 cup (125 to 250 ml), serves 8
Time in the kitchen: 5 minutes, plus a few hours to chill

1 14-ounce (397 g) can full-fat coconut milk

Put the can of coconut milk in the refrigerator for several hours (or overnight).

When you open the can after it's chilled, scrap off the solid top layer of creamy coconut, careful not to include any of the liquid on the bottom of the can. (Don't waste the liquid left in the can—drink it or add it to a smoothie.)

Whip the coconut cream with an electric mixer until it thickens into a loose whipped cream, about five minutes.

Suggested uses

Dollop on fresh berries, Dark Chocolate Pudding Sauce (page 104), and baked apples.

macronutrient profile (per serving)
2 tbsp (30 ml) per serving

	Grams	Calories	%-Cals
Calories		105	
Fat	11	96	91%
Saturated	9	84	80%
Polyunsaturated	0	1	1%
Monounsaturated	1	5	4%
Carbohydrate	1	6	5%
Dietary Fiber	0		
Protein	1	4	4%

dark chocolate coconut sauce

I make this dessert sauce in small amounts because it's a rich treat, but you can easily double or triple the recipe. Turn this sauce into an amazing chocolate bar by pouring the sauce into a small rimmed pan lined with parchment paper. Sprinkle sea salt on top and freeze until solid.

Makes ¼ cup (60 ml), serves 2
Time in the kitchen: 5 minutes

1 ½ to 2 ounces (42 to 57 g) dark chocolate, finely chopped (about ½ cup (125 ml))

1 to 2 tablespoons (15 to 30 ml) coconut oil

Heat half of the chocolate in the microwave in twenty-five-second increments, until melted.

Vigorously stir in the remaining chocolate until it melts. If it doesn't melt completely, put it in the microwave a few more seconds.

Heat the coconut oil until warm.

Slowly drizzle coconut oil into the chocolate until desired consistency and flavor is reached.

Suggested uses

Drizzle over a bowl of raspberries or macadamia nuts, or use as a dip for strawberries.

macronutrient profile (per serving)
2 tbsp (30 ml) per serving

	Grams	Calories	%-Cals
Calories		72	
Fat	6	57	79%
Saturated	5	42	58%
Polyunsaturated	0	1	2%
Monounsaturated	1	10	14%
Carbohydrate	3	13	18%
Dietary Fiber	1		
Protein	1	2	3%

dark chocolate pudding sauce

An addictive dessert sauce that is dangerously versatile. Avocado makes the sauce thick and creamy (and adds healthy fat), but you won't be able to detect the flavor. Chilled, this sauce thickens into pudding. Or, leave the avocado out and heat the sauce to make the best Primal hot chocolate you've ever had.

Makes 1 cup (250 ml), serves 8
Time in the kitchen: 20 minutes

1 cup (250 ml) coconut milk

1 to 3 pitted dates, coarsely chopped

3 tablespoons (45 ml) unsweetened cocoa powder

½ ripe avocado

1 teaspoon (5 ml) vanilla extract

Bring the coconut milk to a gentle boil in a small pot over medium heat.

Add the dates, boil a few minutes, then turn off the heat and let set for ten minutes to soften the dates.

Pour the coconut milk into a blender and blend for twenty-five seconds so the dates are mostly dissolved in the milk.

Add cocoa powder, avocado, and vanilla, and blend until the sauce is thick and creamy.

Suggested uses

Pour over berries or figs or eat the sauce alone with a dollop of coconut milk whipped cream (page 100).

macronutrient profile (per serving)
2 tbsp (30 ml) per serving

	Grams	Calories	%-Cals
Calories		447	
Fat	31	275	61%
Saturated	23	207	46%
Polyunsaturated	1	9	2%
Monounsaturated	5	41	9%
Carbohydrate	38	152	34%
Dietary Fiber	8		
Protein	5	20	4%

PRIMAL BLUEPRINT HEALTHY SAUCES, DRESSINGS & TOPPINGS **105**

berry-coconut sauce

Ripe berries and creamy coconut milk are meant to be together, as this simple but delicious sauce proves.

Makes 1 cup (250 ml), serves 8
Time in the kitchen: 5 minutes

1 cup (250 ml) berries
½ cup (125 ml) coconut milk

Blend ingredients in a food processor or blender until smooth.

Press through a fine sieve to get rid of the seeds.

Serve warm or cold.

Suggested uses

Stir into a bowl of yogurt and nuts, drizzle over Primal pancakes or fresh fruit.

macronutrient profile (per serving)
2 tbsp (30 ml) per serving

	Grams	Calories	%-Cals
Calories		37	
Fat	3	28	76%
Saturated	3	24	64%
Polyunsaturated	0	1	2%
Monounsaturated	0	1	3%
Carbohydrate	2	8	20%
Dietary Fiber	0		
Protein	0	2	4%

raspberry butter sauce

I make this bright, rich sauce in small amounts and drizzle it over everything from Primal pancakes to grilled pork. Add a pinch of sea salt to the sauce to punch up the flavor.

Makes ¼ cup (60 ml), serves 2
Time in the kitchen: 5 minutes

1 cup (250 ml) raspberries

4 tablespoons (60 ml) unsalted butter, melted and warm

Combine raspberries and warm butter in a blender and blend until smooth, about twenty-five seconds.

Push the sauce through a fine sieve with a spatula or spoon to remove the seeds.

Serve warm.

Suggested uses

Drizzle over shredded coconut for dessert, or use as a savory topping for grilled pork or pan-seared salmon tossed with salad greens.

macronutrient profile (per serving)
2 tbsp (30 ml) per serving

	Grams	Calories	%-Cals
Calories		236	
Fat	24	212	90%
Saturated	15	131	55%
Polyunsaturated	1	9	4%
Monounsaturated	6	54	23%
Carbohydrate	8	30	13%
Dietary Fiber	4		
Protein	1	4	2%

coconut-lime sauce

Both tangy and sweet, use this sauce as a dip for fruit or topping for fresh berries.

Makes ¾ cup (175 ml), serves 6
Time in the kitchen: 5 minutes

½ cup (125 ml) crème fraiche

¼ cup (60 ml) coconut milk

½ teaspoon (2 ml) lime juice, or more to taste

Lime zest for garnish

Whisk all ingredients together in a small bowl. Garnish with lime zest. Serve chilled.

Suggested uses

A dip for apples, skewers of strawberries and blackberries, or a sauce for roasted sweet potatoes.

macronutrient profile (per serving)
2 tbsp (30 ml) per serving

	Grams	Calories	%-Cals
Calories		61	
Fat	6	53	86%
Saturated	4	36	59%
Polyunsaturated	0	2	2%
Monounsaturated	1	9	15%
Carbohydrate	2	6	10%
Dietary Fiber	0		
Protein	1	3	4%

SALAD DRESSING

basic vinaigrette

Let's start with the basics. This vinaigrette is perfect for any salad, any time, anywhere. It has tons of flavor and just the right ratio of oil, vinegar, and seasoning. It also reveals a handy trick: combine the shallot, salt, and pepper with the vinegar ahead of time to dissolve the seasonings and mellow the shallot's bite.

Makes 1 cup (250 ml), serves 8
Time in the kitchen: 15 minutes

1 small shallot, finely chopped

¼ teaspoon (1 ml) salt

¼ teaspoon (1 ml) black pepper

3 tablespoons (45 ml) red wine or sherry vinegar

½ teaspoon (2 ml) Dijon mustard (page 172)

¾ cup (175 ml) extra virgin olive oil

Combine shallot, salt, and pepper with the vinegar in a small bowl. Let sit ten minutes.

Whisk mustard and olive oil into dressing.

macronutrient profile (per serving)

2 tbsp (30 ml) per serving

	Grams	Calories	%-Cals
Calories		184	
Fat	20	182	99%
Saturated	3	25	13%
Polyunsaturated	2	19	10%
Monounsaturated	15	133	72%
Carbohydrate	0	2	1%
Dietary Fiber	0		
Protein	0	0	0%

ranch dressing

What makes this dressing so perfect is its simplicity. It strikes all the right creamy, tangy, and herbaceous notes using just a few ingredients. Start here, and then personalize the dressing by experimenting with additions like fresh dill or garlic, a drizzle of vinegar, or spoonful of homemade mayonnaise (page 178).

Makes 1 cup (250 ml), serves 8
Time in the kitchen: 10 minutes

¾ cup (175 ml) sour cream

¼ cup (60 ml) plus 1 tablespoon (15 ml) buttermilk

¾ teaspoon (4 ml) dried dill

1 teaspoon (5 ml) finely chopped fresh chives

½ teaspoon (2 ml) tamari

¼ teaspoon (1 ml) granulated onion powder

⅛ teaspoon (0.5 ml) black pepper

Pinch of salt

In a large bowl, mix together all ingredients by hand until smooth.

Add more salt to taste if needed.

macronutrient profile (per serving)
2 tbsp (30 ml) per serving

	Grams	Calories	%-Cals
Calories		47	
Fat	4	39	84%
Saturated	3	23	48%
Polyunsaturated	0	1	2%
Monounsaturated	1	10	22%
Carbohydrate	1	5	10%
Dietary Fiber	0		
Protein	1	3	6%

caesar dressing

Romaine lettuce is at its best topped with Caesar dressing. Egg yolks are optional; without them the dressing is just as flavorful, but the texture is lighter and more like vinaigrette. For an even creamier dressing, add ½ cup (125 ml) of finely grated Parmigiano-Reggiano cheese.

Makes 1 cup (250 ml), serves 8
Time in the kitchen: 10 minutes

1 tablespoon (15 ml) red wine vinegar

2 tablespoons (30 ml) lemon juice

4 anchovy fillets, finely chopped then mashed into paste

2 garlic cloves, finely chopped

¼ teaspoon (1 ml) salt

⅛ teaspoon (0.5 ml) black pepper

⅔ cup (160 ml) extra virgin olive oil

2 egg yolks (optional)

Whisk vinegar, lemon juice, anchovies, garlic, salt, and black pepper together until well combined in a small bowl.

Whisk in olive oil and egg yolks.

macronutrient profile (per serving)
2 tbsp (30 ml) per serving

	Grams	Calories	%-Cals
Calories		175	
Fat	19	167	95%
Saturated	3	26	15%
Polyunsaturated	2	18	10%
Monounsaturated	13	118	68%
Carbohydrate	1	3	1%
Dietary Fiber	0		
Protein	1	6	3%

thousand island dressing

Whether it's used as a salad dressing or as a dip for a burger patty, this dressing adds a rich, zingy flavor, and is a classic many can't do without.

Makes 1 cup (250 ml), serves 8
Time in the kitchen: 5 minutes, plus time to make mayo and ketchup

1 teaspoon (5 ml) grated white or yellow onion

1 batch (about ¾ cup (175 ml)) homemade mayonnaise (page 178)

¼ cup (60 ml) homemade Easy Ketchup (page 170)

2 tablespoons (30 ml) finely chopped dill pickle (page 182)

2 teaspoons (10 ml) apple cider vinegar

Grating the onion on the small holes of a box grate, rather than dicing it, helps the flavor blend more evenly into the dressing.

Mix the grated onion with the remaining ingredients in a small bowl.

macronutrient profile (per serving)
2 tbsp (30 ml) per serving

	Grams	Calories	%-Cals
Calories		85	
Fat	8	68	80%
Saturated	1	10	12%
Polyunsaturated	4	36	43%
Monounsaturated	2	17	20%
Carbohydrate	4	16	18%
Dietary Fiber	0		
Protein	0	2	2%

blue cheese vinaigrette

This vinaigrette will satisfy your cravings for creamy blue cheese dressing, even though it has no mayonnaise, sour cream or buttermilk. I use walnut oil in this dressing for its mild nutty flavor; olive oil can taste a little bitter and overpower the blue cheese. If you want the dressing to have more zing, use 2 tablespoons (30 ml) of vinegar and eliminate the water.

Makes 1 cup (250 ml), serves 8
Time in the kitchen: 5 minutes

¼ pound (113 g) blue cheese, crumbled

1 tablespoon (15 ml) white wine vinegar

1 tablespoon (15 ml) water

½ cup (125 ml) walnut oil

¼ teaspoon (1 ml) black pepper

1 tablespoon (15 ml) chopped parsley

Blend everything, except parsley, in a blender until smooth, about thirty seconds. Pour dressing into a bowl and mix parsley in by hand.

macronutrient profile (per serving)
2 tbsp (30 ml) per serving

	Grams	Calories	%-Cals
Calories		**173**	
Fat	**142**	**160**	**92%**
Saturated	4	35	20%
Polyunsaturated	9	79	45%
Monounsaturated	4	38	22%
Carbohydrate	**0**	**2**	**1%**
Dietary Fiber	0		
Protein	**3**	**12**	**7%**

dairy-free green goddess dressing

Green Goddess dressing is a classic typically made with sour cream and mayo. The most important ingredient in Green Goddess, though, is the herbs, which I generously add to this dairy-free version. Don't worry too much about measuring exact amounts of the herbs—the more the better. Just grab a handful and use cooking shears to snip them into the food processor.

Makes 1 cup (250 ml), serves 8
Time in the kitchen: 10 minutes

½ avocado

¼ cup (60 ml) coconut milk

3 tablespoons (45 ml) freshly squeezed lemon juice

1 garlic clove, finely chopped

2 anchovy fillets, finely chopped

½ cup (125 ml) coarsely chopped parsley

¼ cup (60 ml) coarsely chopped fresh basil

1 tablespoon (15 ml) coarsely chopped fresh tarragon

¼ teaspoon (1 ml) salt

½ cup (125 ml) extra virgin olive oil

Blend the first nine ingredients in the food processor until combined. With the blade running, pour in the oil and process until the dressing thickens and the herbs are finely chopped.

macronutrient profile (per serving)
2 tbsp (30 ml) per serving

	Grams	Calories	%-Cals
Calories		160	
Fat	17	149	93%
Saturated	3	30	19%
Polyunsaturated	2	15	9%
Monounsaturated	11	97	61%
Carbohydrate	2	8	5%
Dietary Fiber	1		
Protein	1	4	2%

bacon dressing

Warm bacon dressing is especially good over dark greens like spinach and kale. For a breakfast salad, top the greens with a fried egg.

Makes ½ cup (125 ml), serves 4
Time in the kitchen: 15 minutes

4 bacon slices

Extra virgin olive oil as needed

1 tablespoon (15 ml) sherry vinegar

1 tablespoon (15 ml) finely chopped parsley

Fry the bacon in a skillet over medium heat. Remove the cooked bacon from the pan and set aside.

Pour the bacon fat into a bowl—you'll need 3 tablespoons (45 ml) of fat. If there isn't enough, add olive oil.

Whisk together the fat/oil, vinegar, and parsley.

Crumble or chop the bacon into small pieces. Whisk half the bacon crumbles into the dressing. Use the rest as garnish for the salad.

This dressing is best when slightly warm, so use immediately, or put back in the skillet and heat it gently before pouring over a salad.

macronutrient profile (per serving)
2 tbsp (30 ml) per serving

	Grams	Calories	%-Cals
Calories		76	
Fat	7	63	83%
Saturated	2	14	18%
Polyunsaturated	1	7	9%
Monounsaturated	4	36	47%
Carbohydrate	0	1	1%
Dietary Fiber	0		
Protein	3	12	16%

tarragon dressing

Used in small amounts, tarragon's anise-like flavor is delicate and mysterious. This aromatic dressing is especially good in salads topped with chicken or salmon.

Makes 1 cup (250 ml), serves 8
Time in the kitchen: 10 minutes, plus time to hard boil eggs

2 hard-boiled eggs

1 tablespoon (15 ml) finely chopped shallot

3 tablespoons (45 ml) sherry vinegar

1 teaspoon (5 ml) Dijon mustard (page 172)

¼ teaspoon (1 ml) salt

2 teaspoons (10 ml) finely chopped fresh tarragon leaves

½ cup (125 ml) extra virgin olive oil

1 teaspoon (5 ml) water

In a food processor, blend the egg and shallot until smooth, about twenty seconds.

Blend in vinegar, mustard, salt, and tarragon.

With the blade running, pour in the olive oil, then the water, until the dressing slightly thickens.

macronutrient profile (per serving)
2 tbsp (30 ml) per serving

	Grams	Calories	%-Cals
Calories		145	
Fat	15	137	94%
Saturated	2	21	15%
Polyunsaturated	2	16	11%
Monounsaturated	11	96	66%
Carbohydrate	0	2	1%
Dietary Fiber	0		
Protein	2	7	4%

rosemary dressing

Adding fresh herbs is an easy way to change the flavor of vinaigrette. The invigorating flavor of rosemary dominates this one. Try it on a salad topped with ground or thinly sliced lamb.

Makes 1 cup (250 ml), serves 8
Time in the kitchen: 5 minutes

2 teaspoons (10 ml) finely chopped fresh rosemary

1 garlic clove, finely chopped

3 tablespoons (45 ml) red wine vinegar

¼ teaspoon (1 ml) salt

¾ cup (175 ml) extra virgin olive oil

Combine first four ingredients in a small bowl then whisk in olive oil.

macronutrient profile (per serving)
2 tbsp (30 ml) per serving

	Grams	Calories	%-Cals
Calories		183	
Fat	20	182	100%
Saturated	3	25	14%
Polyunsaturated	2	19	10%
Monounsaturated	15	133	73%
Carbohydrate	0	1	0%
Dietary Fiber	0		
Protein	0	0	0%

mint dressing

The aroma alone will make you salivate over this dressing. It's a no-holds barred flavor explosion: minty, spicy, and tangy. Fantastic over steak salad.

Makes ½ cup (125 ml), serves 4
Time in the kitchen: 10 minutes

½ cup (125 ml) coarsely chopped fresh mint

3 green onions, coarsely chopped

1 tablespoon (15 ml) coarsely chopped fresh, peeled ginger

2 tablespoons (30 ml) lime juice

2 teaspoons (10 ml) seeded and finely chopped jalapeño pepper

Pinch of salt

½ cup (125 ml) extra virgin olive oil or coconut oil

Put first six ingredients in a blender and pulse a few times. Remove the center of the lid and with the blade running, drizzle in the oil. Blend until smooth.

This dressing is best eaten the day it's made, as the color will fade when refrigerated for too long.

macronutrient profile (per serving)
2 tbsp (30 ml) per serving

	Grams	Calories	%-Cals
Calories		379	
Fat	41	367	97%
Saturated	6	52	14%
Polyunsaturated	4	38	10%
Monounsaturated	30	266	70%
Carbohydrate	3	10	3%
Dietary Fiber	1		
Protein	1	2	1%

basil-lime dressing

A tart and tangy dressing, light and refreshing, and incredibly aromatic.

Makes 1 cup (250 ml), serves 8
Time in the kitchen: 5 minutes

Combine all ingredients in a blender. Blend until smooth.

¼ cup (60 ml) lime juice

½ cup (125 ml) coconut oil

1 to 2 garlic cloves

½ teaspoon (2 ml) ground cumin

¼ teaspoon (1 ml) salt ·

⅛ teaspoon (0.5 ml) black pepper

Handful of coarsely chopped basil leaves

macronutrient profile (per serving)
2 tbsp (30 ml) per serving

	Grams	Calories	%-Cals
Calories		127	
Fat	14	123	96%
Saturated	12	106	83%
Polyunsaturated	0	2	2%
Monounsaturated	1	7	5%
Carbohydrate	1	4	3%
Dietary Fiber	0		
Protein	0	1	0%

basil-oil dressing

Basil oil has an eye-catching bright green color, and the pure, peppery flavor of basil. Drizzle it plain over seafood or vegetables, or use it to make salad dressings like the one here.

Basil Oil

Makes 1 cup (250 ml)

Ice water

1 teaspoon (5 ml) salt

3 handfuls fresh basil leaves

1 cup (250 ml) extra virgin olive oil

Set a large bowl of ice water next to the stove.

In a separate pot, bring 8 cups of water and a teaspoon of salt to a boil. Add basil leaves and boil for twenty-five seconds. Drain the leaves and then put them into the bowl of cold water. Drain again and then squeeze the leaves with your hands to remove as much water as possible. You'll end up with just a small handful of leaves.

In a blender, purée the leaves with the extra virgin olive oil for two minutes, or until completely smooth.

Pour the basil oil through a fine mesh sieve over a bowl. The oil will drip out very slowly—let this happen undisturbed for about an hour. Don't press on the leaves or the oil will become cloudy. The oil can be stored for one month in an airtight container in the refrigerator.

Basil Oil Dressing

Makes ½ cup (125 ml), serves 8
Time in the kitchen: 15 minutes, plus 1 hour to strain oil

1 tablespoon (15 ml) balsamic or white wine vinegar

2 garlic cloves, finely chopped or pressed

¼ teaspoon (1 ml) salt

½ cup (125 ml) basil oil

Mix together vinegar, garlic, and salt in a small bowl then whisk in oil.

macronutrient profile (per serving)
2 tbsp (30 ml) per serving

	Grams	Calories	%-Cals
Calories		243	
Fat	27	243	100%
Saturated	4	34	14%
Polyunsaturated	3	26	11%
Monounsaturated	20	178	73%
Carbohydrate	0	0	0%
Dietary Fiber	0		
Protein	0	0	0%

basil-berry dressing

Contrast the pleasantly sweet and fruity flavor of this dressing with strips of savory steak or pork over mixed baby greens. If you eat dairy, then drizzle Basil-Berry dressing over salads topped with fresh goat cheese.

Makes ½ cup (125 ml), serves 4
Time in the kitchen: 10 minutes

½ cup (125 ml) blackberries

½ teaspoon (2 ml) honey

2 tablespoons (30 ml) balsamic vinegar

¼ cup (60 ml) coconut oil or extra virgin olive oil

1 tablespoon (15 ml) finely chopped basil

Combine the blackberries, honey, and vinegar in a blender on high for ten seconds.

With the blade running, slowly drizzle the oil into the blender until the mixture is slightly thickened and smooth, about twenty seconds.

Strain the dressing through a fine mesh sieve into a small bowl to remove the seeds.

Sprinkle in the basil and mix with a fork to combine.

macronutrient profile (per serving)
2 tbsp (30 ml) per serving

	Grams	Calories	%-Cals
Calories		138	
Fat	14	122	88%
Saturated	2	16	11%
Polyunsaturated	2	14	10%
Monounsaturated	10	88	64%
Carbohydrate	4	15	11%
Dietary Fiber	1		
Protein	0	1	1%

raspberry dressing

Although you can buy raspberry vinegar, making it at home is easy. It gives salad dressing a fruity, tangy flavor. Raspberries are actually quite low in sugar and high in vitamin C and antioxidants, so I throw a few fresh berries into this dressing as well to give it more sweetness.

Raspberry Vinegar

Makes 1 cup (250 ml)

1 cup (250 ml) red wine vinegar

1 cup (250 ml) frozen raspberries (defrosted and drained of most liquid) or 4 cups (1 L) fresh raspberries

Combine the vinegar and raspberries in a bowl. Cover and put in a cool location like a kitchen pantry. Let the raspberries soak for three days. Taste to decide if your vinegar is done—you can let the berries flavor the vinegar for up to two weeks.

Mash the raspberries into the vinegar, then strain vinegar through a fine mesh sieve.

Raspberry Dressing

Makes 1 cup (250 ml), serves 8
Time in the kitchen: 10 minutes, plus 3 days to macerate raspberries in vinegar

3 tablespoons (45 ml) raspberry vinegar

6 fresh raspberries

¼ teaspoon (1 ml) Dijon mustard (page 172)

¼ teaspoon (1 ml) salt

¾ cup (175 ml) extra virgin olive oil

Blend vinegar, raspberries, mustard, and salt in a food processor or blender until smooth. With the blade running, slowly add oil until well blended.

For a different flavor, try coconut oil or walnut oil in place of olive oil.

macronutrient profile (per serving)
2 tbsp (30 ml) per serving

	Grams	Calories	%-Cals
Calories		225	
Fat	20	183	82%
Saturated	3	25	11%
Polyunsaturated	2	20	9%
Monounsaturated	15	133	59%
Carbohydrate	10	40	18%
Dietary Fiber	2		
Protein	0	2	1%

coconut-cilantro dressing

Equally as good over salad as it is over grilled steak or roasted vegetables, this aromatic, creamy dressing adds an incredible amount of flavor to every meal.

Makes ½ cup (125 ml), serves 4
Time in the kitchen: 10 minutes

1 cup (250 ml) cilantro leaves, coarsely chopped

1 garlic clove

¼ cup (60 ml) extra virgin olive oil or coconut oil

1 tablespoon (15 ml) sesame oil

1 tablespoon (15 ml) almond butter

¼ cup (60 ml) coconut milk

⅛ teaspoon (0.5 ml) salt

2 teaspoons (10 ml) lime juice

Combine all ingredients in a blender until smooth.

macronutrient profile (per serving)
2 tbsp (30 ml) per serving

	Grams	Calories	%-Cals
Calories		212	
Fat	22	200	94%
Saturated	5	47	22%
Polyunsaturated	4	32	15%
Monounsaturated	13	115	54%
Carbohydrate	2	7	3%
Dietary Fiber	1		
Protein	1	5	2%

avocado-lime dressing

The avocado in this dressing comes from avocado oil. The flavor is fairly mild, so it's really the spices that stand out. Try this dressing in a taco salad with grilled steak or chicken, tomato, and sliced avocado.

Makes ½ cup (125 ml), serves 4
Time in the kitchen: 5 minutes

1 garlic clove, minced

½ teaspoon (2 ml) chili powder

2 teaspoons (10 ml) cumin seeds, lightly toasted and ground, or 1 teaspoon (5 ml) pre-ground cumin

¼ teaspoon (1 ml) salt

2 tablespoons (30 ml) lime juice

½ cup (125 ml) avocado oil

Whisk all ingredients together in a small bowl.

macronutrient profile (per serving)
2 tbsp (30 ml) per serving

	Grams	Calories	%-Cals
Calories		255	
Fat	28	248	97%
Saturated	3	29	11%
Polyunsaturated	4	34	13%
Monounsaturated	20	176	69%
Carbohydrate	2	6	2%
Dietary Fiber	0		
Protein	0	1	0%

creamy avocado dressing

A whole avocado makes this dressing thick and creamy. Delicious in salads with shrimp, salmon, or chicken.

Makes 1 cup (250 ml), serves 8
Time in the kitchen: 5 minutes

1 avocado, sliced

2 tablespoons (30 ml) lime juice

¼ cup (60 ml) coconut milk

¼ teaspoon (1 ml) salt

2 tablespoons (30 ml) of water or coconut milk

Blend first four ingredients in a blender until smooth. Add water or coconut milk as needed to thin the dressing, about 2 tablespoons.

Add more salt to taste if needed.

macronutrient profile (per serving)
2 tbsp (30 ml) per serving

	Grams	Calories	%-Cals
Calories		47	
Fat	4	37	79%
Saturated	2	16	33%
Polyunsaturated	0	3	7%
Monounsaturated	2	16	33%
Carbohydrate	2	8	17%
Dietary Fiber	1		
Protein	1	2	4%

sesame-coconut dressing

This dressing blends three oils—coconut, sesame, and sunflower—for a balance of flavor. You can jazz this dressing up even more by adding minced garlic, red pepper flakes, or chopped green onion.

Makes ½ cup (125 ml), serves 4
Time in the kitchen: 5 minutes

3 tablespoons (45 ml) unseasoned rice wine vinegar

1 tablespoon (15 ml) plus 1 teaspoon (5 ml) tamari

2 tablespoons (30 ml) coconut oil

2 tablespoons (30 ml) sesame oil

¼ cup (60 ml) cold-pressed , high-oleic or high-stearic sunflower oil

Whisk all ingredients together in a small bowl.

macronutrient profile (per serving)
2 tbsp (30 ml) per serving

	Grams	Calories	%-Cals
Calories		248	
Fat	27	245	99%
Saturated	8	74	30%
Polyunsaturated	12	108	44%
Monounsaturated	6	52	21%
Carbohydrate	0	1	0%
Dietary Fiber	0		
Protein	1	2	1%

lemon-ginger dressing

Bright and lively with spicy kick from the ginger. Try with steak or fish over dark greens, shredded cabbage, or seaweed.

Makes ½ cup (125 ml), serves 4
Time in the kitchen: 10 minutes

½ teaspoon (2 ml) lemon zest

1 teaspoon (5 ml) grated ginger root

2 tablespoons (30 ml) lemon juice

1 tablespoon (15 ml) tamari

1 tablespoon (15 ml) toasted sesame oil

½ cup (125 ml) extra virgin olive oil

To grate the ginger, cut the peel off the root and use the small holes on a cheese grater. To grate lemon zest, run a lemon back and forth against the small holes on a cheese grater, or use a microplane grater.

Whisk together lemon zest, ginger and the remaining ingredients in a small bowl.

macronutrient profile (per serving)
2 tbsp (30 ml) per serving

	Grams	Calories	%-Cals
Calories		281	
Fat	31	275	98%
Saturated	4	38	14%
Polyunsaturated	4	38	14%
Monounsaturated	21	189	67%
Carbohydrate	1	4	1%
Dietary Fiber	0		
Protein	1	2	1%

coconut masala dressing

Who says all salad dressings have to have oil? This super-simple dressing is both light and creamy at the same time. It's great over mixed baby greens and salmon.

Makes ½ cup (125 ml), serves 4
Time in the kitchen: 5 minutes

½ cup (125 ml) coconut milk

2 teaspoons (10 ml) lime juice

1 tablespoon (15 ml) finely chopped cilantro

½ teaspoon (2 ml) cumin

⅛ teaspoon (0.5 ml) garam masala

Pinch of sea salt

Whisk ingredients together in a small bowl.

macronutrient profile (per serving)
2 tbsp (30 ml) per serving

	Grams	Calories	%-Cals
Calories		62	
Fat	6	54	87%
Saturated	5	47	76%
Polyunsaturated	0	1	1%
Monounsaturated	0	2	4%
Carbohydrate	1	5	8%
Dietary Fiber	0		
Protein	1	3	5%

tahini-olive dressing

Especially good over salads made from chopped chicken, tomatoes, and cucumbers, this dressing also makes a great dip for raw veggies.

Makes 1 cup (250 ml), serves 8
Time in the kitchen: 10 minutes

¼ cup (60 ml) tahini

¼ cup (60 ml) water

2 tablespoons (30 ml) extra virgin olive oil

2 tablespoons (30 ml) lemon juice

1 clove of garlic, finely chopped or pressed

¼ teaspoon (1 ml) sea salt

1 tablespoon (15 ml) finely chopped parsley

¼ cup (60 ml) finely chopped Kalamata olives

In a small bowl, whisk together tahini and water then whisk in oil and lemon juice.

Whisk in remaining ingredients.

macronutrient profile (per serving)
2 tbsp (30 ml) per serving

	Grams	Calories	%-Cals
Calories		94	
Fat	9	77	81%
Saturated	1	10	11%
Polyunsaturated	2	20	22%
Monounsaturated	5	43	45%
Carbohydrate	3	12	12%
Dietary Fiber	1		
Protein	2	6	6%

macadamia oil dressing

The sweet, buttery flavor of macadamia nuts dominates this dressing, which is the whole point. You can add more vinegar if you like, but why get in the way of the great macadamia flavor? Try this dressing over a spinach salad topped with shrimp or grilled fish.

Makes 1 cup (250 ml), serves 8
Time in the kitchen: 5 minutes

1 tablespoon (15 ml) sherry vinegar

¼ teaspoon (1 ml) Dijon mustard (page 172)

2 garlic cloves, finely chopped or pressed

¼ teaspoon (1 ml) salt

¾ cup (175 ml) macadamia oil

In a small bowl, mix together first four ingredients then whisk in olive oil.

macronutrient profile (per serving)
2 tbsp (30 ml) per serving

	Grams	Calories	%-Cals
Calories		190	
Fat	21	189	99%
Saturated	3	27	14%
Polyunsaturated	2	14	7%
Monounsaturated	17	149	78%
Carbohydrate	0	1	1%
Dietary Fiber	0		
Protein	0	0	0%

sumac dressing

Sumac is a spice made from the dried and ground berries of a bush native to the Mediterranean and Middle East. The flavor is tart and gives this dressing an added burst of citrus flavor. Use in seafood salads or on greens tossed with fresh herbs like mint and parsley.

Makes 1 cup (250 ml), serves 8
Time in the kitchen: 10 minutes

1 tablespoon (15 ml) ground sumac

3 tablespoons (45 ml) fresh lemon juice

1 tablespoon (15 ml) tahini

¼ teaspoon (1 ml) salt

¾ cup (175 ml) extra virgin olive oil

Combine the sumac and lemon juice. Let set for five minutes. Vigorously whisk in the tahini, salt, and olive oil.

macronutrient profile (per serving)
2 tbsp (30 ml) per serving

	Grams	Calories	%-Cals
Calories		196	
Fat	21	191	97%
Saturated	3	27	14%
Polyunsaturated	3	24	12%
Monounsaturated	15	136	69%
Carbohydrate	1	4	2%
Dietary Fiber	0		
Protein	0	2	1%

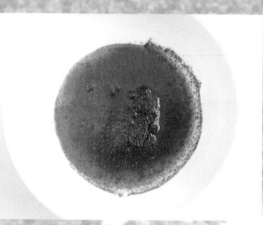

garlic-oil dressing

What can't you use garlic-infused oil for? Good luck finding an answer to that question. Keep garlic infused oil on hand for salad dressings and marinades, drizzling over cooked meat and seafood, or to sauté vegetables.

Garlic Oil

Makes 1 cup (250 ml)

3 cloves of garlic, thinly sliced

1 cup (250 ml) extra virgin olive oil

Thinly sliced garlic, rather than minced, is a better choice for this recipe, since minced garlic is likely to burn.

Combine garlic and oil in a saucepan or pot over medium-low heat. Let it bubble very gently for twenty-five minutes. If the garlic starts to brown too much (heading towards burnt) turn the heat down to low. Strain the garlic out using a fine mesh sieve. Let the oil cool, then store in an airtight container in the refrigerator for up to one month.

Garlic Oil Dressing

Makes ¾ cup (175 ml), serves 6
Time in the kitchen: 15 minutes, plus 30 minutes to make garlic oil

3 tablespoons (45 ml) sherry vinegar

2 tablespoons (30 ml) finely chopped shallot

¼ teaspoon (1 ml) salt

¾ cup (175 ml) garlic oil

Combine the vinegar, shallot, and salt in a small bowl, and let set for ten minutes.

Whisk in the oil until combined.

macronutrient profile (per serving)
2 tbsp (30 ml) per serving

	Grams	Calories	%-Cals
Calories		329	
Fat	36	324	99%
Saturated	5	45	14%
Polyunsaturated	4	35	10%
Monounsaturated	26	237	72%
Carbohydrate	1	4	1%
Dietary Fiber	0		
Protein	0	1	0%

sweet and smoky paprika dressing

Sweet, smoked Spanish paprika has a bold smoky flavor that's key to this dressing. Although good over any type of greens, this bold dressing can really stand up to heavier greens like kale and spinach.

Makes 1 cup (250 ml), serves 8
Time in the kitchen: 5 minutes

3 tablespoons (45 ml) sherry vinegar

1 teaspoon (5 ml) sweet smoked paprika

2 garlic cloves, finely chopped or pressed

¼ teaspoon (1 ml) salt

¾ cup (175 ml) extra virgin olive oil

In a small bowl, combine first four ingredients then whisk in the olive oil.

macronutrient profile (per serving)
2 tbsp (30 ml) per serving

	Grams	Calories	%-Cals
Calories		184	
Fat	20	182	99%
Saturated	3	25	13%
Polyunsaturated	2	19	10%
Monounsaturated	15	133	72%
Carbohydrate	0	2	1%
Dietary Fiber	0		
Protein	0	1	0%

Dips, Condiments and Garnishes

barbecue sauce

Sweet, tangy and delicious barbecue sauce without corn syrup or tons of sugar—just try to find that on the shelves of a grocery store. This Primal sauce is sweetened with just a bit of honey and blackberries, a nutritionally dense fruit packed with antioxidants.

Makes 1 cup (250 ml), serves 8
Time in the kitchen: 50 minutes

2 tablespoons (30 ml) extra virgin olive oil or unsalted butter

1 small red onion, finely chopped

½ cup (125 ml) (about 15) blackberries

2 teaspoons (10 ml) honey

2 tablespoons (30 ml) tomato paste

2 teaspoons (10 ml) apple cider vinegar

1 teaspoon (5 ml) tamari

1 14.5-ounce (411 g) can diced tomatoes in juice

¼ teaspoon (1 ml) salt

¼ teaspoon (1 ml) paprika

½ teaspoon (2 ml) chili powder

¼ teaspoon (1 ml) cayenne pepper (optional)

¼ teaspoon (1 ml) garam masala

¼ to ½ cup (60 to 125 ml) water

Suggested uses

Perfect with burgers, grilled chicken, and grilled pork.

Heat olive oil or butter over medium in a deep pot. Add onion and sauté for ten minutes until soft and just barely browned.

In a food processor, combine onion with next ten ingredients. Process until smooth.

Return to the pot and simmer for twenty-five minutes over medium to medium-low heat, partially covered so it doesn't splatter too much. Stir frequently to prevent the sauce from sticking to the bottom of the pot.

Turn off heat and stir in garam masala and water. At this point the sauce is not going to taste amazing, but don't panic. The next step is crucial to finishing the sauce.

In small batches, pour the sauce into a fine mesh sieve set over a bowl. Push down on the sauce with a spoon, so the solids remain in the sieve and the final liquid sauce is extracted into the bowl. Chill before serving.

macronutrient profile (per serving)
2 tbsp (30 ml) per serving

	Grams	Calories	%-Cals
Calories		71	
Fat	4	33	46%
Saturated	1	5	6%
Polyunsaturated	0	3	5%
Monounsaturated	3	23	32%
Carbohydrate	8	34	47%
Dietary Fiber	2		
Protein	1	5	6%

fresh tomato ketchup

Why bother making homemade ketchup? The delicious flavor of fresh tomatoes easily beats bottled brands and you're avoiding excessive amounts of sugar and other questionable ingredients.

The grape tomatoes (or if you can't find them, cherry tomatoes) are used for their sweet flavor and low-moisture content.

Makes 1 cup (250 ml), serves 8
Time in the kitchen: 50 minutes

1 pound (500 g) grape tomatoes

2 pounds (1 kg) regular tomatoes

½ cup (125 ml) red wine vinegar

1 tablespoon (15 ml) honey

1 teaspoon (5 ml) salt

¼ teaspoon (1 ml) black pepper

Pinch of allspice

½ teaspoon (2 ml) tamari

Cut the grape tomatoes in half. Cut the regular tomatoes in half. Gently squeeze out the seeds and most of the juice and discard, then cut the tomatoes into fourths.

In a large saucepan over medium heat, combine the tomatoes, vinegar, honey, salt and pepper and bring to a boil.

Boil uncovered for thirty-five minutes until the mixture has a thick, jam-like consistency. Stir occasionally, especially towards the end to make sure the tomatoes aren't sticking to the pan.

Purée tomatoes briefly in a food processor, just until smooth, about fifteen seconds.

In small batches, press the tomatoes through a fine sieve, collecting the ketchup in a bowl underneath.

Mix in allspice and tamari. Chill before serving.

Suggested uses

Burgers, sausage, and eggs won't be the same without it.

macronutrient profile (per serving)
2 tbsp (30 ml) per serving

	Grams	Calories	%-Cals
Calories		38	
Fat	0	2	6%
Saturated	0	0	1%
Polyunsaturated	0	1	3%
Monounsaturated	0	0	1%
Carbohydrate	8	30	79%
Dietary Fiber	2		
Protein	1	6	15%

easy ketchup

Whip this flavorful ketchup up even when tomatoes aren't in season. Tangy and slightly sweet with just the right blend of seasonings, it's a dead ringer for the bottled stuff.

Makes 1 cup (250 ml), serves 8
Time in the kitchen: 10 minutes

1 6-ounce (170 g) can tomato paste

¼ cup (60 ml) apple cider vinegar

2 teaspoons (10 ml) honey, or more to taste

1 teaspoon (5 ml) dark or blackstrap molasses

¼ cup (60 ml) water

½ teaspoon (2 ml) salt

1 garlic clove

1 tablespoon (15 ml) finely chopped white or yellow onion

Pinch of allspice or garam masala

Combine all ingredients in a blender at medium-high speed until very smooth.

Chill before serving.

Suggested uses

A dip for burgers and roasted sweet potatoes. Mix with homemade mayo (page 178) to make a "secret sauce."

macronutrient profile (per serving)
2 tbsp (30 ml) per serving

	Grams	Calories	%-Cals
Calories		36	
Fat	0	1	3%
Saturated	0	0	1%
Polyunsaturated	0	0	1%
Monounsaturated	0	0	1%
Carbohydrate	8	31	86%
Dietary Fiber	1		
Protein	1	4	11%

dijon mustard

Mustard is incredibly easy to make. Soak mustard seeds overnight then throw them in a blender; that's pretty much it. The results will blow your mind. To make a milder tasting, less spicy mustard use more yellow seeds. For an aggressively spicy batch, use more brown seeds.

Makes 1 ½ cups (375 ml), serves 24
Time in the kitchen: 10 minutes, plus
24 hours to soak mustard seeds

¼ cup (60 ml) yellow mustard seeds

¼ cup (60 ml) brown mustard seeds

½ cup (125 ml) apple cider vinegar

½ cup (125 ml) water

½ teaspoon (2 ml) salt

Put all of the ingredients in a non-reactive bowl, cover and let sit at room temperature for twenty-four hours.

Pour the entire mixture into a blender. Blend on high until the desired consistency is reached, at least thirty seconds. Keep in mind that the mustard will be grainy and not entirely smooth, since it's made with whole mustard seeds.

Ideally, refrigerate the mustard for a day before serving, so the flavor can really develop. Mustard tends to taste really spicy right after being made, and after a day or two the flavor becomes milder but more complex.

Suggested uses

Spread on burgers, whisk into salad dressings, use in marinades.

macronutrient profile (per serving)
1 tbsp (15 ml) per serving

	Grams	Calories	%-Cals
Calories		274	
Fat	18	162	59%
Saturated	1	9	3%
Polyunsaturated	5	45	16%
Monounsaturated	11	99	36%
Carbohydrate	15	60	22%
Dietary Fiber	6		
Protein	13	52	19%

yellow mustard

This mustard is made with mustard powder instead of whole seeds. There's a big difference between the two. The main benefit of using powder is that it only takes about ten minutes to turn it into mustard.

Makes ½ cup (125 ml), serves 8
Time in the kitchen: 10 minutes

½ cup (125 ml) yellow powdered mustard

¼ cup (60 ml) white wine vinegar

¾ cup (175 ml) water

¼ teaspoon (1 ml) salt

Combine all ingredients in a saucepan over medium heat.

Whisk and stir as the mixture comes to a boil and thickens, eight to ten minutes.

Chill completely before serving.

Suggested uses

For burgers and sausages, and extra flavor for meat rubs and marinades.

macronutrient profile (per serving)
1 tbsp (15 ml) per serving

	Grams	Calories	%-Cals
Calories		34	
Fat	2	20	60%
Saturated	0	1	3%
Polyunsaturated	1	6	17%
Monounsaturated	1	12	37%
Carbohydrate	2	7	21%
Dietary Fiber	1		
Protein	2	7	19%

shallot mustard

A chunky mustard that tastes like a mild Dijon with the sweet flavor of shallot. Serve with pork, burgers, and meatloaf.

Makes 1 ½ cups (375 ml), serves 24
Time in the kitchen: 15 minutes, plus 24 hours to soak mustard seeds

½ cup (125 ml) yellow mustard seeds

½ cup (125 ml) apple cider vinegar

½ cup (125 ml) water

½ teaspoon (2 ml) salt

1 large shallot, thinly sliced

1 teaspoon (5 ml) butter or olive oil

Put all of the ingredients except the shallot and butter/oil in a non-reactive bowl, cover and let sit at room temperature for twenty-four hours.

Over low heat in butter or olive oil, cook the shallot in a saucepan with a lid for eight to ten minutes until soft and lightly browned.

Pour the mustard seed mixture and the shallot into a blender. Blend until desired consistency is reached.

Suggested uses

Spread over pork, whisk into salad dressings, blend into the ground meat for meatloaf.

macronutrient profile (per serving)
1 tbsp (15 ml) per serving

	Grams	Calories	%-Cals
Calories		282	
Fat	18	162	57%
Saturated	1	9	3%
Polyunsaturated	5	45	16%
Monounsaturated	11	99	35%
Carbohydrate	17	68	24%
Dietary Fiber	6		
Protein	13	52	18%

mayonnaise

Homemade mayo only takes a few minutes to make, so I whip up a small batch right before serving it. However, if you want a slightly thicker texture that's more like bottled mayo then refrigerate it for an hour or more before serving.

Using neutral-flavored sunflower oil eliminates the bitter and sometimes overpowering flavor that extra virgin olive oil can give homemade mayo. Only buy cold-pressed (which preserves vitamin E and reduces oxidation), high-oleic or high-stearic sunflower oil. This type of sunflower oil has the same healthy monounsaturated fat found in extra virgin olive oil and lard.

Makes ½ cup (125 ml), serves 4
Time in the kitchen: 10 minutes

1 egg yolk

1 teaspoon (5 ml) lemon juice

¼ teaspoon (1 ml) Dijon mustard (page 172)

1 teaspoon (5 ml) cold water

¼ teaspoon (1 ml) salt

¾ cup (175 ml) cold-pressed high-oleic or high-stearic sunflower oil

Whisk together the egg yolk, lemon juice, mustard, water and salt until frothy.

Whisking constantly, pour the oil in very slowly, only a drop at a time, until the mayonnaise begins to thicken. Once this happens you can add the oil in a thin stream, whisking until completely combined.

Homemade mayo can stay fresh up to a week in the refrigerator, but usually tastes best if eaten within a few days.

Suggested uses

Toss with cooked chicken, use as a base for salad dressing, drizzle over a bacon, lettuce, and tomato salad.

macronutrient profile (per serving)
2 tbsp (30 ml) per serving

	Grams	Calories	%-Cals
Calories		382	
Fat	42	378	99%
Saturated	5	41	11%
Polyunsaturated	27	243	64%
Monounsaturated	9	77	20%
Carbohydrate	0	1	0%
Dietary Fiber	0		
Protein	1	3	1%

lemon aioli

Aioli is essentially garlic mayonnaise, but something magical happens when these ingredients are whisked together that makes it so much more. The bold lemon-garlic flavor and silky texture is a memorable topping for fish and chicken, or as a dip for vegetables. When drizzled lightly over greens it can be a delicious dressing on its own, too.

Makes ½ cup (125 ml), serves 4
Time in the kitchen: 10 minutes

2 egg yolks

1 large garlic clove, very finely chopped or pressed

1 teaspoon (5 ml) cold water

¼ teaspoon (1 ml) salt

¾ cup (175 ml) extra virgin olive oil or cold-pressed high-oleic or high-stearic sunflower oil

2 to 3 tablespoons (30 to 45 ml) lemon juice

Whisk together egg yolks, garlic, water and salt until frothy.

Whisking constantly, pour the oil in very slowly, only a drop at a time, until the aioli begins to thicken. Once this happens you can add the oil in a thin stream, whisking until completely combined.

When all the oil is combined and the aioli is thick, gently whisk in the lemon juice to taste.

Suggested uses

Drizzle over salmon, use as a dip for roasted vegetables or shrimp.

macronutrient profile (per serving)
2 tbsp (30 ml) per serving

	Grams	Calories	%-Cals
Calories		396	
Fat	43	385	97%
Saturated	7	59	15%
Polyunsaturated	5	41	10%
Monounsaturated	31	275	69%
Carbohydrate	1	5	1%
Dietary Fiber	0		
Protein	2	6	2%

dill pickles

These crunchy, perfectly sour pickles are not only easy to make but they're naturally fermented, which means lots of healthy live bacteria.

Makes about 16 pickle spears
Time in the kitchen: 15 minutes, plus 24 to 72 hours for pickles to ferment

2 cups (500 ml) water

2 tablespoons (30 ml) salt

1 teaspoon (5 ml) coriander seeds

6 sprigs fresh dill

4 garlic cloves, peeled

1 pound (about 8) small cucumbers (ideally, Kirby pickling cucumbers, but Persian can work well, too)

Sterilize a canning jar and lid by submerging in boiling water. Air-dry.

Make the brine by combining the water and salt in a small bowl. Let the salt dissolve.

Put the coriander seeds, dill and garlic in the jar.

Wash the cucumbers, trim off the ends and cut the cucumbers in half lengthwise. Stuff them in the jar leaving about 1 inch of space at the top.

Pour the brine over the cucumbers. Place the jar lid loosely on top of the jar, or cover the jar with cheesecloth. Do not seal the jar. Store in a cool, dark place (like a kitchen pantry) for twenty-four to seventy-two hours to ferment. Once the pickles taste good to you, refrigerate.

Without vinegar, pickles don't keep as long, so try to eat them within a week.

Suggested uses

Chop up with tuna or egg salad, serve with pork chops.

macronutrient profile (per serving)
1 pickle per serving

	Grams	Calories	%-Cals
Calories		16	
Fat	0	1	7%
Saturated	0	0	2%
Polyunsaturated	0	0	1%
Monounsaturated	0	0	1%
Carbohydrate	3	12	78%
Dietary Fiber	0		
Protein	1	2	14%

tartar sauce

Now that you know how to make homemade mayo, homemade pickles, and homemade Dijon mustard, you can make homemade tartar sauce. Nearly any type of seafood pairs well with this full-flavored sauce.

Makes ½ cup (125 ml), serves 4
Time in the kitchen: 10 minutes

½ cup (125 ml) homemade
mayonnaise (page 178)

¼ cup (60 ml) finely chopped dill
pickle (page 182)

1 tablespoon (15 ml) drained
capers, coarsely chopped

2 teaspoons (10 ml) grated or very
finely chopped white onion

1 tablespoon (15 ml) finely chopped
fresh parsley

1 teaspoon (5 ml) lemon juice

¼ teaspoon (1 ml) Dijon mustard
(page 172)

Combine all ingredients for the tartar sauce in a small bowl.

Suggested uses

A dip for shrimp and fish, a topping for roasted sweet potatoes, a dressing for coleslaw.

macronutrient profile (per serving)
2 tbsp (30 ml) per serving

	Grams	Calories	%-Cals
Calories		213	
Fat	23	209	98%
Saturated	3	29	14%
Polyunsaturated	14	122	57%
Monounsaturated	6	50	23%
Carbohydrate	1	3	1%
Dietary Fiber	0		
Protein	0	1	0%

pickle relish

Crunchy, fresh and bursting with salty, piquant flavor, this is a relish worth making.

Makes 1 ½ cups (375 ml), serves 12
Time in the kitchen: 10 minutes, plus a few hours to chill

½ cup (125 ml) apple cider vinegar

1 teaspoon (5 ml) yellow or brown mustard seeds

1 teaspoon (5 ml) coriander seeds

8 to 10 dill pickle spears (page 182), chopped into small chunks (about 1 ½ cups (375 ml) of chopped pickle)

⅓ cup finely chopped white or yellow onion

Bring the vinegar, mustard seeds, and coriander seeds to a boil in a non-reactive saucepan. Boil three minutes.

Remove from heat and pour over the pickle and onion.

Let cool to room temperature then refrigerate and chill before serving.

Suggested uses

A garnish for sautéed cabbage and sausage, a topping for pork chops and burgers.

macronutrient profile (per serving)
2 tbsp (30 ml) per serving

	Grams	Calories	%-Cals
Calories		15	
Fat	0	2	10%
Saturated	0	0	2%
Polyunsaturated	0	0	3%
Monounsaturated	0	0	2%
Carbohydrate	3	11	78%
Dietary Fiber	1		
Protein	0	2	11%

spicy relish

Spicy, but not overwhelmingly so. Keep a batch in the fridge and use the relish to top everything from burgers to pork chops to fish.

Makes 1 to 2 cups (250 to 500 ml), serves 16
Time in the kitchen: 20 minutes, plus a few hours to chill

5 cups water

2 red onions, thinly sliced or coarsely chopped

1 cup (250 ml) white vinegar

1 teaspoon (5 ml) salt

1 teaspoon (5 ml) fennel seeds

2 jalapeño peppers, thinly sliced

Bring water to a boil in a small pot.

Add the onion and boil for two minutes. Drain.

Bring the vinegar, salt and fennel seeds to a boil in a small saucepan.

Add the onion and jalapeño and boil for one minute.

Pour everything into a bowl and cool to room temperature.

Chill completely before serving.

Suggested uses

Add a spicy kick to salmon, grilled tuna, and pork roast.

macronutrient profile (per serving)

2 tbsp (30 ml) per serving

	Grams	Calories	%-Cals
Calories		8	
Fat	0	1	7%
Saturated	0	0	1%
Polyunsaturated	0	0	0%
Monounsaturated	0	0	1%
Carbohydrate	2	7	83%
Dietary Fiber	0		
Protein	0	1	10%

scallion-ginger relish

You'll be blown away by how many different uses you'll find for this simple relish with eye-opening flavor. This version is adapted from a recipe by New York Chef David Chang. His recipe uses a lot more ginger plus soy sauce, sherry vinegar and grapeseed oil, which I've substituted with healthier sunflower oil. Spoon it over fish and steak, add it to salads, or use it as a topping for roasted cauliflower or broccoli.

Makes 1 to 2 cups (250 to 500 ml), serves 16
Time in the kitchen: 30 minutes

2 cups (500 ml) thinly sliced scallions

1 tablespoon (15 ml) finely chopped ginger

¼ cup (60 ml) cold-pressed high-oleic or high-stearic sunflower oil

1 teaspoon (5 ml) sesame oil

2 teaspoons (10 ml) unseasoned rice vinegar

¼ teaspoon (1 ml) salt

Combine scallions and ginger in a small bowl.

Whisk together oils, vinegar and salt in a separate bowl. Pour over onions and ginger and mix together.

Let sit at least twenty to thirty minutes, stirring several times throughout.

Over a few days in the refrigerator, the onions will soften and the flavors will meld together more.

Suggested uses

A colorful topping for steak or salmon, or a flavorful add-in to salad.

macronutrient profile (per serving)
2 tbsp (30 ml) per serving

	Grams	Calories	%-Cals
Calories		38	
Fat	4	33	87%
Saturated	0	3	9%
Polyunsaturated	2	21	56%
Monounsaturated	1	7	18%
Carbohydrate	1	4	10%
Dietary Fiber	0		
Protein	0	1	3%

hot harissa sauce

Harissa is a thick hot sauce from Tunisia. The vibrant, fiery flavor is very versatile. It can be used as a condiment on its own or as a rub for meat, a seasoning for dishes like scrambled eggs or to give homemade mayo a kick. The chiles used to make harissa are dried and can be found in many grocery stores.

Makes 1 cup (250 ml), serves 8
Time in the kitchen: 35 minutes

6 New Mexico chiles, stemmed and seeded (about 2 ounces)

6 guajillo chiles, stemmed and seeded (about 2 ounces)

½ teaspoon (2 ml) coriander seeds or ground coriander ·

½ teaspoon (2 ml) caraway seeds or ground caraway

¼ teaspoon (1 ml) cumin seeds or ground cumin

1 teaspoon (5 ml) salt

3 garlic cloves, finely chopped

3 tablespoons (45 ml) extra virgin olive oil

1 tablespoon (15 ml) lemon juice

Put chiles into a bowl. Cover with boiling hot water and let sit until softened, about twenty minutes.

In a dry skillet over medium heat, toast the coriander, caraway and cumin seeds for several minutes until fragrant and lightly toasted. Transfer spices to a coffee grinder and grind into a fine powder. Skip these steps if using ground spices.

Drain chiles and transfer to a blender. Add the ground spices, salt, garlic, olive oil, and lemon juice. Blend at medium speed, stopping occasionally to stir and scrape down the sides of the bowl, until the paste is very smooth. This will take two to five minutes, depending on how powerful your blender is.

Store in an airtight container in the refrigerator.

Suggested uses

Stir into beef stew, smear onto chicken before roasting, spread onto cooked lamb or goat.

macronutrient profile (per serving)
2 tbsp (30 ml) per serving

	Grams	Calories	%-Cals
Calories		56	
Fat	5	46	83%
Saturated	1	7	12%
Polyunsaturated	1	5	8%
Monounsaturated	4	34	61%
Carbohydrate	2	8	14%
Dietary Fiber	0		
Protein	0	2	3%

hot sauce

If you've never made hot sauce before, this basic but delicious recipe will show you how easy it is. Guajillo and arbol chiles are both dried. The amounts here make a moderately spicy sauce. You can play around with the quantities to make the sauce even milder or screamin' hot.

Makes 1 cup (250 ml), serves 8
Time in the kitchen: 30 minutes

2 ounces (about 7) guajillo chiles, stemmed and seeded

4 arbol chiles, stemmed and seeded

4 garlic cloves

¾ cup (175 ml) apple cider vinegar

½ teaspoon (2 ml) ground cumin

1 ½ teaspoon (7.5 ml) salt

¼ teaspoon (1 ml) smoked paprika

Water, as needed

Put chiles into a bowl, cover with boiling hot water and let sit until softened, about twenty minutes. Drain.

Put the chiles in a blender with the garlic, vinegar, cumin, salt and paprika. Blend until very smooth.

Add water (start with ¼ cup (60 ml)) as necessary to help the sauce blend and to make the texture thinner if that's how you like your hot sauce. You can also add more vinegar for a tangier sauce. Store in the refrigerator.

Suggested uses

Serve with eggs, a bowl of ground meat and avocado, or fajitas.

macronutrient profile (per serving)
2 tbsp (30 ml) per serving

	Grams	Calories	%-Cals
Calories		25	
Fat	0	1	4%
Saturated	0	0	0%
Polyunsaturated	0	1	2%
Monounsaturated	0	0	1%
Carbohydrate	5	20	80%
Dietary Fiber	1		
Protein	1	4	16%

red pepper hot sauce

This spicy sauce also has a sweet, garlicky flavor. Instead of using sugar, a red bell pepper adds the sweetness. Make your first batch using only a few Thai red chile peppers then add more once you know you can handle it. It's a good idea to wear latex gloves while handling the peppers. Touching a hot pepper then wiping your eyes is not something you want to experience.

Makes ½ cup (125 ml), serves 4
Time in the kitchen: 20 minutes

1 tablespoon (15 ml) extra virgin olive oil

6 garlic cloves, coarsely chopped

1 small shallot, coarsely chopped

3 Thai red chile peppers, seeded, stems removed, and coarsely chopped

1 red bell pepper, stemmed and seeded and coarsely chopped

1 tablespoon (15 ml) fish sauce

3 tablespoon (45 ml) unseasoned rice vinegar

Warm the oil in a pot over medium heat. Sauté the garlic, shallot, chiles and red pepper for five to seven minutes until soft.

Transfer to a blender and add fish sauce and vinegar. Purée until as smooth as possible.

Cool the sauce, uncovered, then cover tightly and refrigerate for a few days to let the flavor develop before using.

Suggested uses

Stir into mayo or ketchup for condiments with attitude, drizzle over a seafood salad.

macronutrient profile (per serving)
2 tbsp (30 ml) per serving

	Grams	Calories	%-Cals
Calories		67	
Fat	4	32	47%
Saturated	1	5	7%
Polyunsaturated	1	5	7%
Monounsaturated	3	23	34%
Carbohydrate	7	29	44%
Dietary Fiber	1		
Protein	2	6	9%

olive gremolata

Gremolata is a topping made from parsley, garlic and lemon zest. This version adds olives for even more flavor. Sprinkle over braised meats (try it with pot roast), fish, roasted chicken, and roasted vegetables, after they've been cooked.

Makes ½ cup (125 ml), serves 4
Time in the kitchen: 10 minutes

½ cup (125 ml) pitted kalamata or green olives, coarsely chopped

¼ cup (60 ml) finely chopped fresh parsley

1 teaspoon (5 ml) lemon zest

1 small garlic clove, finely chopped or pressed

Combine the ingredients in a small bowl.

Mash gently with a fork to blend.

Suggested uses

Sprinkle over grilled sardines, rub into a pork roast before or after it cooks, throw in a skillet with a fillet of fish.

macronutrient profile (per serving)
2 tbsp (30 ml) per serving

	Grams	Calories	%-Cals
Calories		11	
Fat	1	7	63%
Saturated	0	1	10%
Polyunsaturated	0	1	6%
Monounsaturated	1	7	63%
Carbohydrate	1	3	28%
Dietary Fiber	1		
Protein	0	1	9%

bacon chive butter

Flavored butter, also known as compound butter, is one of the quickest ways to add extra flavor to a meal. Melt pats of flavored butter over any type of cooked meat, vegetables, or seafood for instant flavor. Keep flavored butter in your refrigerator (it stays fresh about a week), and you can easily turn a plain chicken breast, fish fillet, or steamed veggies into a memorable meal.

Makes 1 cup (250 ml) of butter, serves 8
Time in the kitchen: 30 minutes

4 slices of bacon

2 sticks (230 g) unsalted butter, cut into small chunks

¼ cup (60 ml) finely chopped chives

Cook the bacon using your favorite method. Baking bacon is one of the easiest. Heat oven to 400 °F (200 °C) and lay bacon slices on a rimmed baking sheet covered with parchment paper. The paper will keep the bacon from sticking. Bake for seventeen to twenty-five minutes, until bacon reaches desired crispiness.

Allow bacon to cool. Crumble or cut bacon into tiny pieces.

Combine the bacon, butter, and chives in the food processor until smooth, or use a fork to mash ingredients together in a bowl.

To store, press the butter into a bowl, or wrap the butter in a large piece of parchment paper or plastic wrap and roll the butter into a log.

Refrigerate the butter until solid then slice as needed. The butter can also be frozen for several months.

macronutrient profile (per serving)
2 tbsp (30 ml) per serving

	Grams	Calories	%-Cals
Calories		232	
Fat	25	223	96%
Saturated	15	136	59%
Polyunsaturated	1	10	4%
Monounsaturated	7	61	26%
Carbohydrate	0	2	1%
Dietary Fiber	0		
Protein	2	8	3%

Suggested uses

Melt over an omelet, scallops, or a steak.

blueberry chutney

Vibrant in color and flavor, this naturally sweet chutney is also tangy and just a bit savory.

Makes 1 ½ cups (375 ml), serves 12
Time in the kitchen: 10 minutes

2 cups (500 ml) blueberries

⅓ cup (75 ml) finely chopped red onion

2 tablespoons (30 ml) apple cider vinegar

Pinch of cinnamon

Pinch of sea salt

Combine all ingredients in a small pot or saucepan over medium heat.

Bring to a boil; boil for three to five minutes.

Cool completely before serving.

If you'd like a thicker chutney, you can add arrowroot or tapioca starch (page 7).

Suggested uses

Spoon over pork or turkey, or mix with full-fat yogurt for a sweet and savory dessert.

macronutrient profile (per serving)
2 tbsp (30 ml) per serving

	Grams	Calories	%-Cals
Calories		18	
Fat	1	1	4%
Saturated	0	0	0%
Polyunsaturated	0	0	2%
Monounsaturated	0	0	0%
Carbohydrate	48	16	90%
Dietary Fiber	8		
Protein	3	1	6%

sweet potato bacon dip

Bacon gives this dip a savory flavor that tones down the sweetness of the potatoes. If you like, add even more bacon for garnish. Consider serving this dip as a side dish for the holidays.

Makes 1 cup (250 ml), serves 8
Time in the kitchen: 20 minutes, plus time to microwave or roast potatoes

2 sweet potatoes, roasted or microwaved until soft

2 to 4 slices of bacon

1 small shallot, finely chopped

¼ teaspoon (1 ml) smoked paprika

Fresh chives for garnish

Pinch of salt

Peel the potatoes and slice into chunks or rounds. Set aside.

In a large frying pan, cook the bacon until slightly crispy. Remove the bacon from the pan.

Add the shallot and sweet potato to the pan and cook in the bacon fat until the shallot is lightly browned.

Scrape the remaining fat, potato, and shallot into a food processor. Add the paprika and salt, and blend until smooth.

Crumble in the bacon and garnish with chives. Add more salt to taste if needed.

Serve warm or cold.

Suggested uses

A dip for Primal crackers, or a side for pork chops or turkey.

macronutrient profile (per serving)
2 tbsp (30 ml) per serving

	Grams	Calories	%-Cals
Calories		49	
Fat	2	16	32%
Saturated	1	6	11%
Polyunsaturated	0	2	5%
Monounsaturated	1	7	14%
Carbohydrate	6	25	51%
Dietary Fiber	1		
Protein	2	9	17%

roasted cauliflower dip

Roasting cauliflower gives it an amazing caramelized flavor. This dip is so good and has so much flavor that you might want to just eat it as a side dish with a spoon.

Makes 1 cup (250 ml), serves 8
Time in the kitchen: 1 hour

1 head of cauliflower, cut in half, cored, and then thinly sliced

¼ cup (60 ml) extra virgin olive oil

½ teaspoon (2 ml) ground cumin

1 tablespoon (15 ml) tahini

1 tablespoon (15 ml) lemon juice

1 tablespoon (15 ml) chopped parsley

Pinch of salt

Preheat the oven to 450 °F (230 °C).

Spread the cauliflower out in a large rimmed baking pan or two pans if needed—try to keep the cauliflower in a single layer.

Coat cauliflower with olive oil and cumin and lightly salt. Roast for forty-five minutes. Don't stir, or the cauliflower won't brown as nicely.

Scrape the cauliflower into a food processor or blender. Add tahini, lemon juice and parsley. Blend until desired consistency is reached.

Add more salt to taste if needed.

Suggested uses

A dip for Primal crackers, or a side for pot roast and pork loin.

macronutrient profile (per serving)
2 tbsp (30 ml) per serving

	Grams	Calories	%-Cals
Calories		96	
Fat	8	72	75%
Saturated	1	10	11%
Polyunsaturated	1	10	11%
Monounsaturated	5	48	50%
Carbohydrate	4	17	18%
Dietary Fiber	2		
Protein	2	7	7%

artichoke dip

The creaminess in this dairy-free dip comes partly from blended almonds, but also from the naturally soft texture of artichokes hearts. Go ahead and add Parmigiano-Reggiano if you want to make the dip cheesy, but this dip doesn't really need it.

Makes 2 cups (500 ml), serves 16
Time in the kitchen: 10 minutes

2 14-ounce (396 g) cans of artichoke hearts in water (reserve liquid)

½ cup (125 ml) raw blanched slivered almonds

2 tablespoons (30 ml) homemade mayonnaise (page 178)

In a blender, combine just four of the artichoke hearts with 4 tablespoons (60 ml) of the liquid from the artichoke can, plus the almonds and mayonnaise. Be patient, scrape down the sides occasionally and pulse until very smooth.

Add remaining artichoke hearts. Pulse a few times so they're chopped but still chunky.

Add salt to taste.

Scrape into a serving bowl, or gently heat the dip then serve.

Suggested uses

A dip for raw veggies and chicken skewers, or a side for halibut.

macronutrient profile (per serving)
2 tbsp (30 ml) per serving

	Grams	Calories	%-Cals
Calories		47	
Fat	3	26	56%
Saturated	0	3	6%
Polyunsaturated	1	11	23%
Monounsaturated	1	11	24%
Carbohydrate	4	15	31%
Dietary Fiber	1		
Protein	2	7	14%

onion dip

Often made from a dry packet of onion soup mix, this version is actually made with real onion. Imagine that! It's a favorite dip to serve with raw veggies. If you want to tone down the tanginess of the sour cream, then add a few tablespoons of homemade mayonnaise (page 178) to the dip as well.

Makes 1 cup (250 ml), serves 8
Time in the kitchen: 35 minutes

1 tablespoon (15 ml) butter

1 tablespoon (15 ml) extra virgin olive oil

1 cup (250 ml) finely chopped white or yellow onion

1 tablespoon (15 ml) balsamic vinegar, plus ¼ teaspoon

1 cup (250 ml) sour cream

Pinch of salt

Over medium-low heat, warm butter and olive oil in a small saucepan.

Add the onion and sauté twenty minutes until onions are soft and caramelized—be careful that they don't burn.

Add 1 tablespoon (15 ml) balsamic vinegar and cook another five minutes.

Let the onions cool then mix together with the sour cream and remaining ¼ teaspoon (1 ml) of balsamic vinegar.

The dip really needs a few hours—or even overnight—to reach its full flavor potential. After some time, the sweet onion flavor will take over in a delicious way.

Suggested uses

A dip for raw veggies, or a topping for steak and pot roast.

macronutrient profile (per serving)
2 tbsp (30 ml) per serving

	Grams	Calories	%-Cals
Calories		77	
Fat	127	55	71%
Saturated	24	27	35%
Polyunsaturated	3	3	4%
Monounsaturated	20	23	29%
Carbohydrate	34	17	22%
Dietary Fiber	3		
Protein	10	5	6%

PRIMAL BLUEPRINT HEALTHY SAUCES, DRESSINGS & TOPPINGS

sundried tomato dip

The intense flavor of sundried tomatoes makes a rich dip that gets more addictive with every bite. You can also spread this over cooked pork and chicken for a main course.

Makes ¾ cup (175 ml), serves 6
Time in the kitchen: 10 minutes

½ cup (125 ml) oil-packed sun-dried tomatoes, drained

1 roasted red bell pepper

1 garlic clove

¼ cup (60 ml) walnuts or other nut

1 tablespoon (15 ml) red wine vinegar

¼ cup (60 ml) extra virgin olive oil

1 green onion, chopped for garnish

Water, as needed

If you'd like to roast the pepper yourself, place a whole red bell pepper directly over a flame on a gas stove or grill, or under a broiler. Roast until all side of the pepper are charred. Place the pepper in a bowl covered with plastic wrap (or a plate) to help steam the skin off. When the pepper cools, cut it open, and scrape out all the seeds. Use your hands to peel and rub the blackened skin off.

Pulse sun-dried tomatoes, red pepper, garlic, nuts, and vinegar in a food processor or blender to finely chop.

With the blade running, add oil, and blend until the oil is mixed in and the dip is smooth. If needed, add 1 to 2 tablespoons (15 to 30 ml) of water to make blending easier and thin the consistency of the dip out a little.

Garnish with green onions.

Suggested uses

A dip for raw veggies, or topping for pork and steak.

macronutrient profile (per serving)
2 tbsp (30 ml) per serving

	Grams	Calories	%-Cals
Calories		146	
Fat	14	122	84%
Saturated	2	15	10%
Polyunsaturated	4	32	22%
Monounsaturated	8	71	48%
Carbohydrate	5	18	12%
Dietary Fiber	2		
Protein	2	6	4%

chicken liver dip

This dip is almost pâté, but takes less time to make and has less butter. With bacon and parsley, it's a tasty way to take advantage of the protein, vitamins and minerals found in liver.

Makes 1 ½ cups (375 ml), serves 12
Time in the kitchen: 35 minutes

2 pieces of bacon

½ yellow onion, finely chopped

1 shallot, finely chopped

2 pounds (1 kg) chicken livers, white membranes cut off

2 tablespoons (30 ml) butter

¼ cup (60 ml) finely chopped parsley

Fry the bacon in a large skillet over medium heat. Remove when done and set aside. When the bacon cools, crumble it into small pieces.

Turn the heat down to medium-low and add the onion and shallot, sautéing in the bacon fat until soft and tender, about five minutes.

Bring heat back up to medium, add the chicken livers to the pan, and cook until just barely pink in the middle, eight to twelve minutes.

Add the butter. When it melts, scrape everything into a food processor with the parsley and bacon bits.

Blend until smooth.

Scrape into a serving bowl and chill before serving.

Suggested uses

Spread on Primal crackers, eat with a spoon, or use as a dip for carrots and celery.

macronutrient profile (per serving)
2 tbsp (30 ml) per serving

	Grams	Calories	%-Cals
Calories		162	
Fat	9	83	51%
Saturated	4	32	19%
Polyunsaturated	2	17	10%
Monounsaturated	3	23	14%
Carbohydrate	1	5	3%
Dietary Fiber	0		
Protein	19	74	46%

Spice Blends

barbecue rub

Instead of adding sugar to this barbecue rub, cinnamon provides the sensation of sweetness.

Makes ½ cup (125 ml)
Time in the kitchen: 30 minutes

1 teaspoon (5 ml) yellow mustard seeds

2 teaspoons (10 ml) cumin seeds, lightly toasted

1 teaspoon (5 ml) coriander seeds, lightly toasted

¼ cup (60 ml) paprika

1 teaspoon (5 ml) garlic powder

1 ½ teaspoon (7.5 ml) cinnamon

½ teaspoon (2 ml) black pepper

Grind mustard, cumin, and coriander seeds into a fine powder.

Combine all the ingredients for the rub in a small bowl.

Suggested uses

Blend into hamburger meat, rub down roasts, steak, and chicken before grilling.

macronutrient profile

	Grams	Calories	%-Cals
Calories		178	
Fat	6	54	30%
Saturated	1	6	4%
Polyunsaturated	3	27	15%
Monounsaturated	2	18	10%
Carbohydrate	25	100	56%
Dietary Fiber	14		
Protein	6	24	13%

cajun rub

A spicy-hot blend that can be rubbed onto meat or seafood. You can also sprinkle it into homemade mayonnaise (page 178) to make a spicy dip for shrimp.

Makes ½ cup (125 ml)
Time in the kitchen: 30 minutes

2 tablespoons (30 ml) paprika

2 tablespoons (30 ml) dried oregano

1 tablespoon (15 ml) dried thyme

1 teaspoon (5 ml) cayenne pepper

1 tablespoon (15 ml) ground black pepper

2 teaspoons (10 ml) garlic powder

1 teaspoon (5 ml) onion powder

Combine all the ingredients for the rub in a small bowl.

Suggested uses

Rub onto a pork roast or ribs, mix with olive oil and coat shrimp before grilling, sprinkle onto eggs.

macronutrient profile

	Grams	Calories	%-Cals
Calories		163	
Fat	3	27	17%
Saturated	1	7	4%
Polyunsaturated	1	9	6%
Monounsaturated	0	4	2%
Carbohydrate	29	116	71%
Dietary Fiber	14		
Protein	5	20	12%

chili powder

The smoky, earthy, spicy flavor of this chili powder will quickly convince you to always make your own. You can experiment with any variety of dried pepper that you like, but this blend is close to perfection.

Makes ½ cup (125 ml)
Time in the kitchen: 30 minutes

3 ancho chiles

3 chipotle chiles

3 guajillo chiles

2 arbol chiles

Cut off the steams of the chiles and shake out all the seeds.

Roast the peppers in a dry skillet, or in an oven heated to 300 °F for five minutes until chiles darken slightly and blister.

Let cool, then crumble or cut into small pieces. Grind into a fine powder.

Suggested uses

Use as a seasoning for chili, fajitas, and taco meat.

macronutrient profile

	Grams	Calories	%-Cals
Calories		105	
Fat	1	9	9%
Saturated	0	1	1%
Polyunsaturated	0	3	3%
Monounsaturated	0	0	0%
Carbohydrate	20	80	76%
Dietary Fiber	5		
Protein	4	16	15%

taco seasoning

This homemade blend of spices has more kick and flavor than store-bought taco seasoning.

Makes ½ cup (125 ml)
Time in the kitchen: 30 minutes

2 tablespoons (30 ml) cumin seeds, lightly toasted

1 teaspoon (5 ml) coriander seeds, lightly toasted

2 tablespoons (30 ml) chili powder

1 tablespoon (15 ml) garlic powder

1 tablespoon (15 ml) dried oregano

⅛ teaspoon (0.5 ml) allspice

Grind cumin and coriander seeds into a fine powder.

Combine all the ingredients for the seasoning in a small bowl.

Suggested uses

Sprinkle onto ground meat, over sautéed onions and peppers, and rub into chicken.

macronutrient profile

	Grams	Calories	%-Cals
Calories		182	
Fat	6	54	30%
Saturated	1	6	3%
Polyunsaturated	2	18	10%
Monounsaturated	2	18	10%
Carbohydrate	25	100	55%
Dietary Fiber	11		
Protein	7	28	15%

indian spice blend

This is a simple blend inspired by the complex flavors found in the Indian spice blend garam masala.

Makes ½ cup (125 ml)
Time in the kitchen: 30 minutes

¼ cup (60 ml) coriander seeds, lightly toasted

2 tablespoons (30 ml) cumin seeds, lightly toasted

1 tablespoon (15 ml) black peppercorns, lightly toasted

4 cardamom pods, seeded

4 cloves

2 teaspoons (10 ml) ground ginger

½ teaspoon (2 ml) cinnamon

Grind coriander, cumin, peppercorns, cardamom seeds and cloves into a fine powder.

Combine all the ingredients for the spice blend in a small bowl.

Suggested uses

Rub into lamb and pork before cooking, sprinkle into stews.

macronutrient profile

	Grams	Calories	%-Cals
Calories		215	
Fat	7	63	29%
Saturated	1	6	3%
Polyunsaturated	1	9	4%
Monounsaturated	5	45	21%
Carbohydrate	31	124	58%
Dietary Fiber	16		
Protein	7	28	13%

green curry paste

This version of Thai green curry paste has a flavor that's fresher and more vibrant than jarred curry paste from a store. The paste stays fresh for about two weeks in the refrigerator, so keep some on hand and you'll find endless uses for it.

Makes ½ cup (125 ml)
Time in the kitchen: 30 minutes

1 stalk lemongrass, thinly sliced

1 to 3 Thai green chiles, stems removed

1 shallot, coarsely chopped

4 garlic cloves

2-inch (5 cm) piece of fresh ginger root, peeled and sliced

½ cup (125 ml) coarsely chopped fresh cilantro

½ cup (125 ml) coarsely chopped fresh basil

½ teaspoon (2 ml) ground cumin

1 teaspoon (5 ml) ground coriander

2 tablespoons (30 ml) fish sauce

Juice of 1 lime

2 tablespoons (30 ml) coconut milk, plus additional if needed

To slice lemongrass, first cut off the bulb and peel away the tough outer layers to reveal a tender stalk. This pale, yellowish-green stalk should be easy to slice.

Place all ingredients in a blender. Blend until the ingredients form a smooth paste.

If needed, add more coconut milk to make the ingredients easier to blend.

Adjust seasonings to your liking, adding more hot chiles for extra spiciness, lime for more tartness, and so forth.

macronutrient profile

	Grams	Calories	%-Cals
Calories		157	
Fat	1	9	6%
Saturated	0	2	1%
Polyunsaturated	0	4	2%
Monounsaturated	0	4	2%
Carbohydrate	31	124	79%
Dietary Fiber	4		
Protein	6	24	15%

Suggested uses

Rub it into meat before it cooks, heat it in a pan with leftover red meat, or mix with coconut milk for a quick sauce.

coconut spice blend

The more I cook with this sweet and spicy blend, the more uses I find for it. The more I cook with this blend, the more uses I find for it. It smells incredible and has a unique, sweet and spicy flavor.

Makes 1 cup (250 ml)
Time in the kitchen: 30 minutes

1 cup (250 ml) unsweetened coconut flakes

1-inch (2.5 cm) piece of peeled ginger root, finely chopped

2 garlic cloves, coarsely chopped

1 tablespoon (15 ml) finely chopped shallot

Blend all ingredients in a food processor on medium speed for one minute.

Store in the refrigerator.

Suggested uses

Sauté in a pan with oil, then meat or veggies, sprinkle lightly on cooked fish, purée with coconut milk, and use as a base for stews.

macronutrient profile

	Grams	Calories	%-Cals
Calories		424	
Fat	24	216	51%
Saturated	22	198	47%
Polyunsaturated	0	2	0%
Monounsaturated	1	9	2%
Carbohydrate	49	196	46%
Dietary Fiber	9		
Protein	3	12	3%

za'atar spice blend

Za'atar is a vibrantly colored and flavored Middle Eastern spice blend that can be sprinkled on just about anything. This recipe for Za'atar is heavy on sumac, which has a bold, citrusy flavor.

Makes ½ cup (125 ml)
Time in the kitchen: 30 minutes

1 tablespoon (15 ml) sesame seeds, lightly toasted

2 tablespoons (30 ml) fresh or dried thyme

1 tablespoon (15 ml) dried oregano

¼ cup (60 ml) sumac

Grind the sesame seeds briefly to break them up a little bit.

Combine all the ingredients for the spice blend in a small bowl.

Suggested uses

Sprinkle on cooked fish or roasted vegetables, rub into lamb or pork before it cooks.

macronutrient profile

	Grams	Calories	%-Cals
Calories		97	
Fat	5	45	46%
Saturated	1	9	9%
Polyunsaturated	2	18	19%
Monounsaturated	2	18	19%
Carbohydrate	10	40	41%
Dietary Fiber	6		
Protein	3	12	12%

chimichurri spice blend

Inspired by South American chimichurri sauce made with fresh herbs, garlic, olive oil, and vinegar. This dried blend is a great seasoning for beef and lamb, especially if mixed with olive oil and salt and rubbed on before cooking.

Makes 1 cup (250 ml)
Time in the kitchen: 30 minutes

½ cup (125 ml) dried oregano

¼ cup (60 ml) dried parsley

¼ cup (60 ml) dried thyme

1 tablespoon (15 ml) dried minced garlic

1 tablespoon (15 ml) cumin seeds, lightly toasted

2 teaspoons (10 ml) ground coriander

½ teaspoon (2 ml) red pepper flakes

Combine all the ingredients for the spice blend in a small bowl.

Suggested uses

Use a seasoning for roasts, rub onto a whole chicken with butter, sprinkle on fajitas.

macronutrient profile

	Grams	Calories	%-Cals
Calories		314	
Fat	6	54	17%
Saturated	1	9	3%
Polyunsaturated	2	18	6%
Monounsaturated	2	18	6%
Carbohydrate	53	212	68%
Dietary Fiber	27		
Protein	12	48	15%

french spice blend

Loosely based on the traditional Herbes de Provence blend, this aromatic combination can be sprinkled on pork, chicken or fish. It's also a surprisingly nice addition sprinkled on meatloaf. You can make the blend from store-bought dried herbs, or better yet, from fresh herbs you dry yourself.

Makes ½ cup (125 ml)
Time in the kitchen: 30 minutes

¼ cup (60 ml) dried thyme

¼ cup (60 ml) dried parsley

2 tablespoons (30 ml) dried marjoram

1 tablespoon (15 ml) dried tarragon

1 teaspoon (5 ml) dried rosemary

1 teaspoon (5 ml) fennel seeds

1 teaspoon (5 ml) dried lavender flower

Combine all the ingredients for the spice blend in a small bowl.

Suggested uses

Sprinkle on sautéed eggplant and bell pepper, sprinkle over goat cheese, rub into a pork roast before cooking.

macronutrient profile

	Grams	Calories	%-Cals
Calories		192	
Fat	4	36	19%
Saturated	1	9	5%
Polyunsaturated	1	9	5%
Monounsaturated	1	5	2%
Carbohydrate	33	132	69%
Dietary Fiber	11		
Protein	6	24	13%

nori salt blend

This blend includes salt because it's more of a seasoning that you can leave out on the table, rather than something to add to food before it cooks. Sprinkled over cooked meat, seafood and vegetables this Japanese-inspired blend is subtle but addicting.

Makes ½ cup (125 ml)
Time in the kitchen: 30 minutes

4 roasted nori sheets, ripped into small pieces

1 teaspoon (5 ml) Sichuan peppercorns, lightly toasted

2 tablespoons (30 ml) sesame seeds, lightly toasted

1 teaspoon (5 ml) sea salt

Grind the nori sheets and peppercorns into fine powder.

Grind the sesame seeds briefly, or you can leave them whole.

Combine all the ingredients for the blend in a small bowl.

Suggested uses

Season cooked beef skewers, roasted carrots and steamed, grated cauliflower rice.

macronutrient profile

	Grams	Calories	%-Cals
Calories		121	
Fat	9	81	67%
Saturated	1	9	7%
Polyunsaturated	4	36	30%
Monounsaturated	3	27	22%
Carbohydrate	6	24	20%
Dietary Fiber	3		
Protein	4	16	13%

dried herb blend

Instead of using store-bought dry herbs, which usually have no flavor or aroma, buy (or pick) fresh herbs and then dry them yourself. You'll be amazed by how much more flavor they have.

Makes ½ cup (125 ml)
Time in the kitchen: 30 minutes

1 cup (250 ml) fresh rosemary leaves

½ cup (125 ml) fresh sage leaves, finely chopped

¼ cup (60 ml) fresh thyme leaves

6 garlic cloves, coarsely chopped

Spread the herbs and garlic out in one layer on a baking pan or plate, and let sit uncovered for three days.

Once dried, you can pulse the herbs and garlic in a grinder to make the texture finer if you like, or leave it chunky.

Suggested uses

Mix with butter and rub down a chicken, season root vegetables before they roast, sprinkle lightly on cooked pork.

macronutrient profile

	Grams	Calories	%-Cals
Calories		115	
Fat	3	27	23%
Saturated	1	9	8%
Polyunsaturated	0	4	3%
Monounsaturated	0	4	3%
Carbohydrate	19	76	66%
Dietary Fiber	9		
Protein	3	12	10%

lemon herb blend

This fresh blend doesn't keep long, so plan to refrigerate it and use within a few days. You can sprinkle it over anything you're sautéing, or blend it with butter and rub it over chicken. It's also fantastic rubbed into a roast (beef or pork) before you cook it.

Makes ½ cup (125 ml)
Time in the kitchen: 30 minutes

4 garlic cloves

1 teaspoon (5 ml) salt

½ cup (125 ml) fresh herbs (such as parsley), finely chopped

1 teaspoon (5 ml) ground black pepper or 1 teaspoon (5 ml) whole peppercorns, coarsely chopped

Zest from 2 lemons

Finely chop garlic cloves on a cutting board and sprinkle the salt on top.

Use the flat side of a large knife to mash and grind the salt into the cloves until the garlic turns into a paste.

Mix the garlic paste in a bowl with the fresh herb, pepper and lemon zest.

Suggested uses

Stuff into a whole fish, toss with shrimp, or rub into flank steak before cooking.

macronutrient profile

	Grams	Calories	%-Cals
Calories		44	
Fat	0	0	0%
Saturated		0	0%
Polyunsaturated		0	0%
Monounsaturated		0	0%
Carbohydrate	9	36	82%
Dietary Fiber	3		
Protein	2	8	18%

fennel blend

The intense licorice-like flavor and aroma of fennel dominates this blend. A little bit goes a long way. Sprinkle over fish, pork, or chicken before cooking.

Makes ½ cup (125 ml)
Time in the kitchen: 30 minutes

2 tablespoons (30 ml) coriander seeds, lightly toasted

1 teaspoon (5 ml) whole black peppercorns or blend of peppercorns

½ cup (125 ml) fennel seeds, lightly toasted

Grind coriander seeds and peppercorns into a fine powder.

Grind fennel seeds into a fine powder, or you can pulse them a few times so that some texture remains.

Combine all the ingredients for the blend in a small bowl.

Suggested uses

Sprinkle inside a whole fish before cooking, rub into a lamb shoulder before roasting, sprinkle lightly on cooked pork chops.

macronutrient profile

	Grams	Calories	%-Cals
Calories		245	
Fat	9	81	33%
Saturated	0	4	1%
Polyunsaturated	1	9	4%
Monounsaturated	6	54	22%
Carbohydrate	32	128	52%
Dietary Fiber	23		
Protein	9	36	15%

mushroom powder

If you like mushrooms, you'll love mushroom powder. Sprinkle mushroom powder over vegetables and eggs, add it to soups, sauces, and gravy, or use it to season meatloaf or burgers.

Makes 1 cup (250 ml)
Time in the kitchen: 30 minutes

1 ½ ounces (42 g) dried mushrooms (such as porcini and chantarelle)

1 tablespoon (15 ml) dried herbs (optional)

Break or cut dried mushrooms into small pieces.

Grind into a fine powder.

Combine mushroom powder and dried herbs in a small bowl.

Suggested uses

Season steaks before cooking, mix with melted butter and pour over salmon before cooking, sprinkle in a frittata.

macronutrient profile

	Grams	Calories	%-Cals
Calories		20	
Fat	0	0	0%
Saturated		0	0%
Polyunsaturated		0	0%
Monounsaturated		0	0%
Carbohydrate	4	16	80%
Dietary Fiber	2		
Protein	1	4	20%

MARINADES

basil-lime marinade

The amazing aroma of this marinade will make you want to drink it with a straw. Use on beef, pork, chicken...heck, use it for anything!

Makes marinade for 1 to 2 pounds (0.5 to 1 kg) of meat
Time in the kitchen: 30 minutes

Juice of 1 lime

3 tablespoons (45 ml) coconut oil

2 garlic cloves

2 handfuls fresh basil leaves

½ teaspoon (2 ml) salt

¼ teaspoon (1 ml) black pepper

Combine all ingredients in a blender until fairly smooth.

macronutrient profile

	Grams	Calories	%-Cals
Calories		405	
Fat	41	369	91%
Saturated	35	315	78%
Polyunsaturated	1	9	2%
Monounsaturated	2	18	4%
Carbohydrate	7	28	7%
Dietary Fiber	1		
Protein	2	8	2%

spicy cilantro marinade

Spicy and zesty. A favorite with red meat and lamb.

Makes marinade for 1 to 2 pounds (0.5 to 1 kg) of meat
Time in the kitchen: 30 minutes

1 cup (250 ml) loosely packed cilantro leaves

¼ cup (60 ml) extra virgin olive oil or coconut oil

2 tablespoons (30 ml) red wine vinegar

2 garlic cloves

2 jalapeño peppers, sliced

½ teaspoon (2 ml) salt

Combine all ingredients in a blender until fairly smooth.

macronutrient profile

	Grams	Calories	%-Cals
Calories		510	
Fat	54	486	95%
Saturated	7	63	12%
Polyunsaturated	6	54	11%
Monounsaturated	39	351	69%
Carbohydrate	5	20	4%
Dietary Fiber	1		
Protein	1	4	1%

ginger-garlic marinade

The spiciness that comes from ginger is both eye-opening and soothing at the same time. Use this marinade with seafood, chicken, or red meat.

Makes marinade for 1 to 2 pounds (0.5 to 1 kg) of meat
Time in the kitchen: 30 minutes

1 5-inch piece ginger, peeled and thinly sliced

3 tablespoons (45 ml) coconut oil

¼ cup (60 ml) unseasoned rice vinegar

3 garlic cloves

½ teaspoon (2 ml) salt

¼ teaspoon (1 ml) freshly ground black pepper

Combine all ingredients in a blender until fairly smooth.

macronutrient profile

	Grams	Calories	%-Cals
Calories		**441**	
Fat	41	369	84%
Saturated	35	315	71%
Polyunsaturated	1	9	2%
Monounsaturated	2	18	4%
Carbohydrate	16	64	15%
Dietary Fiber	2		
Protein	2	8	2%

lemon-garlic marinade

It's hard to go wrong with a garlic-infused marinade. You can use this to season just about anything.

Makes marinade for 1 to 2 pounds (0.5 to 1 kg) of meat
Time in the kitchen: 30 minutes

3 tablespoons (45 ml) extra virgin olive oil

Juice of 1 lemon

8 garlic cloves

½ teaspoon (2 ml) salt

Combine all ingredients in a blender until fairly smooth, or finely chop the garlic cloves and whisk together with other ingredients in a small bowl.

macronutrient profile

	Grams	Calories	%-Cals
Calories		421	
Fat	41	369	88%
Saturated	6	54	13%
Polyunsaturated	4	36	9%
Monounsaturated	30	270	64%
Carbohydrate	11	44	10%
Dietary Fiber	1		
Protein	2	8	2%

lemon-pepper marinade

The tart citrus and spicy black pepper in this marinade can make even the blandest chicken breast taste great. You can also use this marinade for seafood, just don't marinate for too long; twenty minutes tops. Acidic liquid like lemon juice can actually "cook" seafood and you'll end up with ceviche.

Makes marinade for 1 to 2 pounds (0.5 to 1 kg) of meat

Time in the kitchen: 30 minutes

3 tablespoons (45 ml) extra virgin olive oil

¼ cup (60 ml) lemon juice

1 shallot, thinly sliced

1 tablespoon (15 ml) black

peppercorns, coarsely chopped with a knife

½ teaspoon (2 ml) salt

Combine all ingredients for the marinade in a small bowl.

macronutrient profile

	Grams	Calories	%-Cals
Calories		417	
Fat	41	369	88%
Saturated	6	54	13%
Polyunsaturated	4	36	9%
Monounsaturated	30	270	65%
Carbohydrate	11	44	11%
Dietary Fiber	2		
Protein	1	4	1%

balsamic-rosemary marinade

Lamb and beef both benefit from a soak in this marinade. It's also a nice marinade for vegetables like eggplant and red pepper.

Makes marinade for 1 to 2 pounds (0.5 to 1 kg) of meat

Time in the kitchen: 30 minutes

¼ cup (60 ml) balsamic vinegar

1 tablespoon (15 ml) tamari

2 tablespoons (30 ml) extra virgin olive oil

1 teaspoon (5 ml) mustard

3 sprigs of rosemary, leaves stripped from stem

Combine all ingredients for the marinade in a small bowl.

macronutrient profile

	Grams	Calories	%-Cals
Calories		**320**	
Fat	**28**	**252**	**79%**
Saturated	4	36	11%
Polyunsaturated	3	27	8%
Monounsaturated	20	180	56%
Carbohydrate	**14**	**56**	**18%**
Dietary Fiber	1		
Protein	**3**	**12**	**4%**

mustard marinade

Pork is a favorite meat for this marinade, although poultry is great too.

Makes marinade for 1 to 2 pounds (0.5 to 1 kg) of meat

Time in the kitchen: 30 minutes

⅓ cup (75 ml) Dijon mustard (page 172)

Handful of fresh parsley or tarragon, finely chopped

1 tablespoon (15 ml) apple cider vinegar

2 tablespoons (30 ml) extra virgin olive oil

Combine all ingredients for the marinade in a small bowl.

macronutrient profile

	Grams	Calories	%-Cals
Calories		331	
Fat	31	279	84%
Saturated	4	36	11%
Polyunsaturated	4	36	11%
Monounsaturated	22	198	60%
Carbohydrate	8	32	10%
Dietary Fiber	5		
Protein	5	20	6%

coconut-almond marinade

Soak any type of meat in this sweet, mellow marinade.

Makes marinade for 1 to 2 pounds (0.5 to 1 kg) of meat

Time in the kitchen: 30 minutes

1 cup (250 ml) coconut milk

Juice of 1 lime

¼ cup (60 ml) raw, unsalted, smooth almond butter

2 garlic cloves, finely chopped

Handful of parsley or cilantro leaves, coarsely chopped

½ teaspoon (2 ml) salt

Whisk together all ingredients for the marinade in a small bowl.

macronutrient profile

	Grams	Calories	%-Cals
Calories		939	
Fat	83	747	80%
Saturated	45	405	43%
Polyunsaturated	9	81	9%
Monounsaturated	23	207	22%
Carbohydrate	28	112	12%
Dietary Fiber	9		
Protein	20	80	9%

aromatic thai marinade

Versatile, flavorful and deliciously aromatic.

Makes marinade for 1 to 2 pounds (0.5 to 1 kg) of meat
Time in the kitchen: 30 minutes

Small handful fresh basil leaves

Small handful cilantro

4 garlic cloves, finely chopped

2 tablespoons (30 ml) fish sauce

Juice of 1 lime

¼ cup (60 ml) coconut oil

Combine all ingredients for the marinade in a blender and blend until herbs are finely chopped.

macronutrient profile

	Grams	Calories	%-Cals
Calories		**543**	
Fat	**55**	**495**	**91%**
Saturated	47	423	78%
Polyunsaturated	1	9	2%
Monounsaturated	3	27	5%
Carbohydrate	**9**	**36**	**7%**
Dietary Fiber	1		
Protein	**3**	**12**	**2%**

indian marinade

The yogurt in this marinade tenderizes meat over the course of a few hours. It works especially well with chicken breast and lamb. Just make sure to brush off most of the yogurt before you cook the meat.

Makes marinade for 1 to 2 pounds (0.5 to 1 kg) of meat

Time in the kitchen: 30 minutes

1 tablespoon (15 ml) Indian spice blend (page 222)

2 garlic cloves, finely chopped

½ white or yellow onion, coarsely chopped

½ cup (125 ml) of whole fat plain yogurt

1 tablespoon (15 ml) lime juice

1 teaspoon (5 ml) salt

Combine all ingredients for the marinade in a small bowl.

macronutrient profile

	Grams	Calories	%-Cals
Calories		149	
Fat	5	45	30%
Saturated	3	27	18%
Polyunsaturated	0	2	1%
Monounsaturated	2	18	12%
Carbohydrate	20	80	54%
Dietary Fiber	4		
Protein	6	24	16%

southwest marinade

Beef is a natural for this marinade, but it's also a great way to season raw vegetables before you throw them on the grill.

Makes marinade for 1 to 2 pounds (0.5 to 1 kg) of meat

Time in the kitchen: 30 minutes

1 tablespoon (15 ml) taco seasoning (page 221)

½ teaspoon (2 ml) salt

2 tablespoons (30 ml) lime or orange juice

¼ cup (60 ml) extra virgin olive oil, or other oil of choice

Combine all ingredients for the marinade in a small bowl.

macronutrient profile

	Grams	Calories	%-Cals
Calories		523	
Fat	55	495	95%
Saturated	8	72	14%
Polyunsaturated	6	54	10%
Monounsaturated	40	360	69%
Carbohydrate	6	24	5%
Dietary Fiber	2		
Protein	1	4	1%

mediterranean marinade

Lamb and beef love a good soak in this herbal marinade.

Makes marinade for 1 to 2 pounds (0.5 to 1 kg) of meat

Time in the kitchen: 30 minutes

⅓ cup (75 ml) red wine vinegar or red wine

3 tablespoon (45 ml) extra virgin olive oil

2 garlic cloves, coarsely chopped

1 tablespoon (15 ml) dried oregano

1 tablespoon (15 ml) fresh or dried thyme

2 rosemary sprigs, leaves stripped from stem

½ teaspoon (2 ml) salt

Combine all ingredients for the marinade in a small bowl.

macronutrient profile

	Grams	Calories	%-Cals
Calories		409	
Fat	41	369	90%
Saturated	6	54	13%
Polyunsaturated	4	36	9%
Monounsaturated	30	270	66%
Carbohydrate	9	36	9%
Dietary Fiber	4		
Protein	1	4	1%

jamaican marinade

Make this robust marinade as spicy or mild as you like by adding more or less hot chiles.

Makes marinade for 1 to 2 pounds (0.5 to 1 kg) of meat
Time in the kitchen: 30 minutes

¼ cup (60 ml) coconut oil

2 tablespoons (30 ml) white vinegar

4 green onions

2 or more Scotch bonnet or habanero chiles, stemmed, seeded and coarsely chopped

2 garlic cloves, coarsely chopped

1 tablespoon (15 ml) fresh thyme

1 teaspoon (5 ml) allspice

½ teaspoon (2 ml) salt

Combine all ingredients in a blender until fairly smooth.

macronutrient profile

	Grams	Calories	%-Cals
Calories		579	
Fat	55	495	85%
Saturated	47	423	73%
Polyunsaturated	1	9	2%
Monounsaturated	3	27	5%
Carbohydrate	18	72	12%
Dietary Fiber	5		
Protein	3	12	2%

anchovy paste

The anchovies won't make meat taste fishy, they simply give the natural flavor of the meat a boost. Give it a try with red meat or chicken.

Makes marinade for 1 to 2 pounds (0.5 to 1 kg) of meat
Time in the kitchen: 30 minutes

3 garlic cloves

6 anchovy fillets, drained and patted dry

½ teaspoon (2 ml) salt

¼ cup (60 ml) extra virgin olive oil

2 tablespoons (30 ml) lemon juice

Finely chop garlic and anchovies. Sprinkle with salt and mash into a paste with the flat side of a large knife.

Combine the garlic-anchovy paste with the olive oil and lemon juice in a small bowl.

macronutrient profile

	Grams	Calories	%-Cals
Calories		614	
Fat	58	522	85%
Saturated	9	81	13%
Polyunsaturated	7	63	10%
Monounsaturated	40	360	59%
Carbohydrate	5	20	3%
Dietary Fiber	0		
Protein	18	72	12%

Ingredient Index

F

fennel, 80
    seeds, 188, 227, 231
fish sauce, 196, 223, 242

G

garam masala, 152, 166, 170
garlic, 38, 52, 53, 58, 62, 64, 68, 70, 74, 82, 90, 92, 94, 98, 118, 124, 130, 134, 136, 142, 144, 154, 156, 160, 162, 170, 180, 182, 192, 194, 196, 198, 212, 223, 224, 229, 230, 234, 235, 236, 237, 241, 242, 243, 245, 246, 247
    dried, 226
    powder, 218, 219, 221
ginger
    fresh, 132, 150, 190, 223, 224, 236
    powdered, 222
green bell pepper, 68
green olives, 64, 198
guajillo chile, 192, 194

H

habanero chile, 246
honey, 92, 138, 166, 168
horseradish root, 34

J

jalapeño pepper, 64, 94, 96, 98, 132, 188, 196, 235

K

kalamata olives, 80, 154, 198
ketchup, 120

L

lavender seeds, 227
leeks, 82
lemon, 230
    juice, 30, 32, 78, 84, 86, 118, 124, 150, 154, 158, 178, 180, 192, 198, 206, 237, 238, 247
lemongrass, 223
lime
    juice, 72, 92, 94, 96, 98, 110, 132, 134, 142, 144, 146, 152, 223, 234, 242, 243, 244

M

macadamia nut, 70, 74
    oil, 156
marjoram, 227
mayonnaise, 120, 184, 208
mint, 78, 132
molasses, 170
mushrooms, 38, 48, 50, 232
    dried, 52
    portobello, 52
mustard
    brown seeds, 172, 186
    dijon, 86, 114, 128, 140, 156, 178, 184, 239, 240
    powder, 174
    yellow seeds, 172, 176, 186, 218

N

new mexico chile, 192
nori, 228
nutmeg, 36
nuts
    macadamia, 70, 74
    walnut, 70, 74, 212

O

olive
    green, 64, 198
    kalamata, 80, 154, 198
    oil, 38, 48, 50, 52, 53, 62, 64, 68, 70, 74, 78, 80, 84, 90, 96, 114, 118, 124, 126, 128, 130, 132, 136, 138, 140, 142, 150, 154, 158, 160, 162, 166, 176, 180, 192, 196, 206, 210, 212, 235, 237, 238, 239, 240, 244, 245, 247
onions, 11, 46, 48, 52, 53, 58, 64, 68, 80, 90, 94, 98, 120, 170, 184, 186, 210, 214, 243
    powder, 68, 116, 219
    red, 96, 166, 188, 202
    scallions, 60, 68, 92, 132, 190, 212, 246
orange bell pepper, 68
orange juice, 244
oregano, 52, 53, 58, 64, 68, 226, 219, 221, 225, 245